The First Step

to a

Blissful Marriage

Chris Gbenle and Sharp Ugwuocha

THE FIRST STEP TO A BLISSFUL MARRIAGE
© 2010 Chris Gbenle and Sharp Ugwuocha. All rights reserved.

No part of this book may be reproduced, stored in a retrieval system, or transmitted by any means without the written permission of the author.

First published by AuthorHouse May 2010

ISBN: 978-1-4520-2205-5 (sc)

Reprinted with Authors permission by PRINTECH (EUROPE) LTD July 2010

ACKNOWLEDGEMENT:

We sincerely wish to acknowledge and express our warm gratitude to our families without whose support it would have been impossible to put this book together. The successive groups of students at the pre-marital school offered us a lot of insight into the common challenges faced by Christian people going into marriage. It was a pleasure to work with you all. The Fountain of Love family and the larger Redeemed Christian Church network have been most instrumental to our personal developments.
Most worthy of mention the General Overseer of our mission, Pastor E.A. Adeboye who has been a father indeed to us.

Above all, we say a very big thank YOU to our dear Heavenly Father. It is a great honour to have known YOU and to have been entrusted with this responsibility of sharing those things YOU taught us with others. Thank YOU dear Lord JESUS! We love YOU so much.

Chris Gbenle and Sharp Ugwuocha

The First Step To A Blissful Marriage

NOTES

....
....
....
....
....
....
....
....

CONTENTS

	Page
Acknowledgement	iii
Introduction	vii
Chapter 1	1
ARE THERE RIGHT AND WRONG REASONS FOR GETTING MARRIED?	
Chapter 2	15
BASIC TRUTHS ABOUT CHOICE OF A SPOUSE	
Chapter 3	20
IMPORTANT QUESTIONS TO ASK YOURSELF BEFORE YOU TAKE THE STEP	
Chapter 4	24
WHAT CAN INFLUENCE MY CHOICE?	
The Core Influences	
Chapter 5	28
WHAT CAN INFLUENCE MY CHOICE?	
The Common Issues That Can Make You Pause	
Chapter 6	46
THE PLACE OF MATURITY IN CHOICE OF A SPOUSE	
Chapter 7	56
AMBER/STOP SIGNS BEFORE YOU GO TOO FAR	
Chapter 8	71
THE CHECK-POINTS	
Chapter 9	75
GOD'S LEADING IN KNOWING THE RIGHT PERSON TO MARRY	
Chapter 10	83
THE PROCESS OF CHOOSING A SPOUSE	

Chapter 11	88
CONVICTION	
Chapter 12	91
TO WHAT EXTENT CAN I BE SURE THAT I AM RIGHT?	
Chapter 13	97
WHAT SHOULD I DO WHEN HE/SHE IS NOT WILLING TO MARRY ME?	
Chapter 14	102
MAJOR CHALLENGES OR OBSTACLES TO CHOICE OF WHOM TO MARRY	
Chapter 15	107
HELPFUL AND RECOMMENDED APPROACHES TO PROPOSALS AND RESPONSES	
The First Choice	109
Bibliography	110

INTRODUCTION

Statistically, it is reported that on average one marriage is dissolved for every two that are contracted. This has been the trend in many Western nations and the same pattern is now observable in other nations. The divide is not only getting blurred between the nations but between the secular populace and the Christian community. The spread of this phenomenon amongst non homogenous groups point to the fact that there is possibly a common thread that runs through the groups and it is invariably the thread of global secularisation. It is frequently said these days that we live in a global village and that what happens in one part of the world quickly spreads to other parts. The internet and 24 hours news coverage ensure that we all literally read from the same page. Poorly scrutinised and appraised standards are adopted by many as the norm. It is more of a game of numbers now - 'Everyone is doing it, and I shall not be left behind...' is the new paradigm. Most times the conversations on a Monday morning starts with "...Did you see the program...?" The inquisition is often not to condemn or even put the matter to test, but simply to make it known that 'I am on the train, are you coming along?' The current is so strong that it will take the mighty to stem it and swim in the opposite direction. While still on this point of the global influence of the 'powerful' few on the rather prostrate majority, the role of the media must be mentioned. The reach of the celebrity cult is very long. It stretches right through movies to soap operas and into glossy magazines.

The First Step To A Blissful Marriage

The reality shows and TV contests all silently but powerfully speak into our subconscious about how it should be done. The argument is simply – if the successful people are doing it, it must be okay. This is not to suggest that we have all lost our sense of right and wrong, but that we have abrogated our responsibility to question things. Sparing a little thought would have made it clear that someone who is on his or her fourth failed marriage may not be successful in the true sense of the word after all. **The real test of a person's worth is in his or her marriage. It is quite possible to stage manage other relationships and associations, but it is near impossible to stay married properly to someone for any length of time without the real person coming out.**

So if most young people's lives are patterned after those of the well known faces it might help if we ponder a bit on how these role models run their lives. We may not have to look very far before we see that the number one cause of the failure of these marriages is in how they make the choice of their spouse. I am quite aware that those who influence us most times are not as visible as it has been stated above. It might just be that humble family member or the ordinary classmate or friend, but the effect on our lives are not in any way less profound.

Marriages are failing at an alarming rate! And this can only be put down to one thing – poor understanding and preparation for marriage. The initial choice we make determines the final outcome. The Lord told His people: "... I have set before you life and death, blessing and cursing, therefore choose life that you and your descendants may live." [Deuteronomy 30: 19].

A building is as strong as its foundation.

Introduction

"Whosoever comes to me and hears my sayings, and does them, I will show you to whom he is like: He is like a man who built a house, and dug deep, and laid the foundation on a rock: and when the flood arose, the stream beat vehemently upon that house, and could not shake it: for it was founded upon a rock." [Luke 6: 47 – 48].

Throughout the following chapters you will hear sayings of the Lord; it will serve you well if you do them, just as the Lord advised in the scripture above.

Take good care to lay a solid foundation for your marriage because therein you will find joy.

The First Step To A Blissful Marriage

NOTES

....
....
....
....
....
....

CHAPTER 1

ARE THERE RIGHT AND WRONG REASONS FOR GETTING MARRIED?

Just as a building cannot stand without a good foundation, so is a marriage contracted for the wrong reasons primed for failure.

The motives and the real intentions for entering a marriage relationship often remain undisclosed. The first step towards saving yourself the pain of a failed marriage is to choose to marry for the right reasons and chose the right person with right motives.

It is possible to do the right thing with the right reasons and motives. In fact that is the greatest guarantee for success. Openness and sincerity is however required. You need to be true to yourself. As you look at the items stated below, please do not make excuses for yourself or explain it away. Check your heart and check it again to see if there is anything that is less than perfect lurking there as a reason for wanting to get married to that particular person you are considering to marry.

Wrong Reasons to Get Married

1. To gain influence with the rich and famous

Some people use marriage as a means of getting connected to the rich and famous in the society. Being connected to people of influence is good, but to enter a marriage for the main purpose of gaining influence is to build the marriage on a shaky foundation.

Fame, riches and all the privileges that come with them are subject to change. The only thing that is permanent is change. When influence and connection disappear, the basis for the marriage will also disappear.

Both men and ladies are known to have actively sought and courted the company of the rich and famous, for the singular purpose of entering into a marriage relationship with them or their friend or family. We may all frown at being called gold diggers or opportunists, but in the real sense of it, is that not what you are if your number one reason for wanting to marry a person is to make gains for yourself through their fame or riches?

Making headway in such marriages can be very challenging. The predicament can be likened to being caught between the devil and the deep blue sea. The conditions to opt out are as bad as the challenges of staying in. People in such situations are filled with thoughts of how just a phone call to their benefactors could suddenly bring to an end all the benefits they enjoy. On the other hand the trauma of trying to love somebody they never loved while still acting as if they did could be harrowing too.

2. To Overcome Economic Hardship

Some Christians that come from very poor backgrounds see marriage as a means of getting out of poverty. The focus of a person like that will be to find someone of means who can take good care of them and their family. Often, all other criteria and virtues are secondary. Hence once a marriage proposal comes up particularly from a well-to-do man, the foremost thought in such a person's mind is how their hardship will quickly come to an end by accepting to marry the person even before they get their heads around the objective reasons to accept or not. For some, the method by which the person they are interested in got his money is irrelevant.

This category of people must be distinguished from those whose main drive is greed and love of wealth. Anyone who is in this group will gladly justify his or her position. Such a person's thought process is that the meeting of a wealthy person is an answered prayer and that it is God who is working in their situation. The person will easily tick that as his or her conviction that God is involved. The error in such an approach is not hard to see. There are many wealthy wolves (just as there are poor ones too) out there, and the appearance of a wealthy person in your life may prove nothing.

3. Pressure to escape from difficult home situation

One of the signs of a good family is where freedom is exercised within the bounds of respect, law and order. Also a good sign of maturity is independence within the limits of mutual dependence in a family. Some young Christians who find themselves in homes or family cultures where they feel repressed, somehow hope to escape someday from such home situation through marriage. Indeed they would jump at the prospect of leaving home at the slightest opportunity. The more daring ones may actually prefer to achieve liberty by eloping with a man in the name of marriage. Generally if the desire to be free from family or parents is the strong force pushing someone into a marriage relationship it sometimes end up as a 'frying pan to fire' situation. The possible outcome is that your spouse may see you as desperate and having nowhere to go or no one to turn to.

There are cases however where God is using some difficult situations at home to communicate to a complacent Christian ripe for marriage that it is time for marriage. That is like God saying to the individual that 'it is time to disturb the comfortable, so that the disturbed may be comforted.'

4. Immigration.

Many immigrants in rich and economically developed nations are in most cases restricted in terms of right to work (work permit) or right to reside (residence permit). Some immigrants in a bid to overcome these disadvantages have resorted to marrying citizens of such countries because through such marriages their status would change in terms of right to live and right to work. It is clear that in such circumstances, the motive and reason behind the marriage from the onset is selfish, wrong and far from the real essence of marriage.

This does not mean that all immigrants who have married citizens of developed nations did that for the purpose of staying on in such countries. There are many who married based on God's leading and selfless genuine reasons to people of other cultures and nationalities.

5. Fear.

Fear generally can lead one into bondage. God through the scriptures would always advise 'FEAR NOT'. Some people have been through some rough experiences in their past and now they fear that if a particular person would not marry them, then no one else would ever marry them. Some are slaves to fear.

Some people out of the fear that they are advancing in age have consciously walked into disastrous marriages. Despite the clear sign and feeling that they are walking into a trap, some have been overwhelmed with the fear that if they missed that opportunity to marry, then that is it gone forever and no one else would marry them. Please as a Christian do not move into marriage out of fear of missing your opportunity for life.

6. Means of Appreciation

To say 'thank you' for a favour received is good, but to use your life by agreeing to marry someone you otherwise would not have married, is one 'thank you' a little too many. There are cases where some people ended up marrying those who helped them in one major area or the other just to show their appreciation.

This can occur very subtly in situations in which someone helped you out at a time when you are vulnerable; like in bereavement, schooling period or during a time of serious career setbacks. The feeling of deep gratitude can be easily confused with deep love. Some surviving colleagues of firemen who perished in the World Trade Centre bombing in 2001 in the United States ended up marrying their colleagues' widows whom they were comforting.

These happened before the first anniversary of the death of their colleagues. Some of these may possibly be because of true love, but the possibility exists as well that a lot of mangled emotions are involved.

There is more to marriage than showing appreciation. Choosing to marry a person solely as a means of appreciation is not the best idea.

7. Sexual Pressure

Christians are aware that pre-marital sex is prohibited by the Scripture. However, in some cases it has been seen that the pressure to have sex have pushed some young people into early and wrong marriages just in a bid to justify having it legitimately.

Nowadays, love has been confused with sex. Little wonder, having sex is interpreted as 'making love' and the more romantic two people are, the more we think that they are deeply in love. The ironic truth is that the more romantic our society is becoming, the greater the rates of failed marriages.

It is clear that there is a wrong interpretation of the place of sex in real love and in marriage. Truthfully, sex can be far from love. Though having sex in marriage is not an ungodly thing but entering into marriage with the sole purpose of using marriage as a platform for sex is wrong and dangerous.

People who used marriage as a ticket to have sex would soon discover that they have paid far too much after the marriage start struggling after a little while.

Are There Right and Wrong Reasons For Getting Married? [1]

I was once in a Bible study group of Christian youths comprising of eligible bachelors and spinsters while someone in response to a question said that; if a Christian single person is having problem controlling his or her sexual desires, the fellow should go and marry quickly as suggested by Paul in 1 Corinthians 7: 1-9.

A closer look at this scripture makes it clear that Apostle Paul was not suggesting that marriage should be rushed into just for the purpose of satisfying sexual desire; rather he was instructing his readers in verse 1 that they should avoid ungodly sex, encouraging that everyone should keep to his or her spouse.

In verse 8 again, his message was that self-control is the ultimate answer to ungodly sex and that for the un-married and widows the last resort is that they are allowed to marry if they must.

There is a grace of self-control available for the young Christians who want to keep themselves pure. Here is the big question, if getting married is the ultimate solution to sexual lusts then why is it that some married people are still promiscuous? Allowing the curiosity to have sex to push one into marriage can dull the person's senses in discerning the right choice of a spouse and may lead to serious disappointments afterward.

8. Answer to boredom and loneliness.

Marriage offers a lifetime of companionship and it is not meant to be a quick fix for the occasional loneliness and perennial boredom. I would even suggest that those who consider themselves very lonely and bored would need to deal with that before marriage. Let such people get meaningfully occupied before marriage.

The First Step To A Blissful Marriage

Before Eve, Adam was in the garden as the only human being but we never learnt he complained of loneliness probably because he was pre-occupied with the meaningful business that God assigned him to do.

Marriage should not be used solely as a panacea for loneliness. The essence of marriage goes far beyond just being a solution for boredom and loneliness.

A person can feel bored and lonely in a crowd. So it is in some marriages where the couple offer no real company to one another. Either or both of them may wish that they were not even married in the first place.

There are better ways to ease boredom and loneliness for Christians like using your time in the service of the Lord, joining Church activity groups, engage in some community development programmes or even do more sporting activities.

9. Peer Pressure.

Going into a marriage just because of peer pressure may sound farfetched, but that is actually what some people do. If we will accept that many people including some Christians will always want to follow what is in vogue, then it would be easy to understand why some go into marriage just because it is the fashionable thing to do. Because your mates and peers are getting married is not a good enough reason to enter into marriage. The quest just to belong to the group of 'the married' may lead a believer to compromise on his or her choice of who to marry.

Things are made all the more difficult when your mates and friends flaunt it that they are now different because of their newly acquired status. However, the grace of God is sufficient as you patiently wait for your right time and the right person. Therefore, do not jump into marriage just to prove a point that you are not different or as a reaction to the disrespect received from your mates and friends. You do not have to prove to anybody that you also can get married whenever you wish. This is another wrong reason to start a marriage.

10. Pregnancy.

(a) Unplanned Pregnancy - Some jump into marriage that they would normally not have considered simply because an unplanned pregnancy has resulted. In this case, the accidental pregnancy now becomes the basis for marrying the person. Sadly as it may be, even among some professing Christians, some marriages have been quickly rushed into in a bid to cover up the act of fornication committed. They rather marry a person they are not convinced about, than face the shame of their hypocrisy being uncovered.

In some cultures, it is the parents that would force their daughters to marry the man that got her pregnant because the parents cannot stand the societal shame of pregnancy and child out of wedlock.

(b) Planned Pregnancy – This is about someone who is getting some resistance from the prospective spouse or facing parental objection and then resorts to getting pregnant as a means of breaking the resistance.

In such instances the lady would deliberately become pregnant for a man she desperately wants to marry. A man on the other hand can deceptively impregnate a 'resistant' woman he wants to marry possibly through the use of alcohol or spiking the drink with drugs.

11. Wants a Baby

There are cases where some people are not actually interested in companionship and oneness that is in marriage but rather desperately wants a baby. They have reduced the essence of marriage to just having somebody to legitimately answer the father or mother of their baby or children. This may occur more commonly in communities where single parenthood is frowned at. The interest in the marriage easily disappears when the baby or children have arrived. All attention is then shifted to the child or children who were the main excuse for the marriage.

12. The Glamour of Wedding.

What may endear some people (especially ladies) to marriage is the glamour which goes with the wedding ceremony. The wedding dress, the procession, the confetti, the wedding cake and many more are just too much a temptation for some to resist. When these good things become an obsession, it becomes a struggle for a person to focus properly and see well beyond the wedding and look at the prospect of the marriage failing or succeeding. The requirements for wedding are easier to meet than the ones needed for marriage. Money and possibly some nice looks are the only absolute essentials for a good wedding ceremony. The simple advice is that you should look beyond the wedding ceremony and focus more on what makes a marriage work and blissful. Remember that the wedding ceremony lasts only for a few hours but the marriage is for a lifetime. Please do not for the sake of a few hours of glamour jeopardize your future by marrying the wrong person and thereby sentence yourself to a lifetime of misery.

13. Just to have a caterer/carer

This may sound odd but does happen particularly in communities where a particular gender is seen as the one responsible for the household chores. In other cases, people with underlying health conditions may want to marry just to get someone to take care of them. There is nothing wrong in showing care but if the primary reason for marrying someone is to have the person cater or care for you, then I think it would be better to hire or employ a carer for that purpose.

Candid Advice

Please in order to lay a good marital foundation it will be wise to evaluate the reasons behind your choice of a spouse. Do not get caught up in the unfortunate situation of marrying for the wrong reasons.

Right Reasons to Get Married

1. The desire to help each other be better Christians.

The strong desire to see each other remain in faith in the Lord Jesus Christ and to lead a successful Christian life together as a couple is essential for Christians to marry.

2. Mutual Love

A strong mutual love is essential for a marriage relationship to commence and to thrive well. As will be discussed later, there is a kind of love that goes beyond the strong sexual attraction to the person of opposite sex. It is an unselfish love. Look out for this and be sure it is present before you go ahead into marriage.

3. Sincere Aspiration to share your lives and possessions with each other

If you find it difficult to see yourself sharing all that you have with someone else, possibly to the point of that person calling the shots in your major live decisions, you may probably not be ready yet for marriage. Because marriage is about sharing, it should be expected that you will lose a few things and of course gain some things as well. Such a feeling to share i.e. to lose and yet gain must be strong towards whomsoever you decide to marry.

We have discovered that this kind of feeling is lacking in a good number of those we counsel. They still hold on too much to what is his and what is hers. Please, deal with this matter before you say, 'I do'.

4. Lifetime companionship.

Your spouse should be your best friend. A good companion is one in whose company you feel comfortable. You do not need to talk all the time, but the fact that you are in the same room or house gives you a sense of security and joy. Also your companion is one whom you miss sorely if you are away from one another for a length of time.

5. Willingness to support and help each other fulfil your dreams

Please make sure that your number one 'destiny helper' is your spouse. If you cannot be bothered if this person you are thinking of marrying fulfils her or his dream or not, then you do not have any business considering him or her for marriage. I guess the first question you need to ask yourself is: do I know his or her dream - if he or she has any at all? And the next is: am I able to help him or her advance the dreams or help formulate one, if there is none?

Marriage relationships that are built on these Biblical ideals are complimentary and are often full of respect for God and for one another. Their thoughts are constantly on doing what they believe God made them for.

6. Willingness to be naked before the person and not ashamed

To be open about your past and your present and not feel ashamed is a necessity for a successful marriage. The kind of things people hide from one another during courtship makes one wonder why they would think a marriage based on such disinformation will ever succeed. The details of the lurid past need not be disclosed if you feel uncomfortable about it, but to let your spouse know a few years into your marriage through the press that you are an ex-convict is a cruel breach of trust.

The excuse that: 'if I tell you, you may not marry me...' is no excuse at all. The foundation of deception will only hold a building of deception. You will always need multiple lies to sustain one lie. If you think you will be spurned, or harshly judged by the person you intend to marry when you are open with the person, then without doubt, that person is not meant for you. Go your way and let him or her go his or her way too.

7. You have the conviction that you are meant for each other.

All these points put together in addition to other guidance from God should bring you to the place where you know with a reasonable degree of assurance that this is the person that is meant for you. That is what is often referred to as your conviction in marriage. We will deal with this matter in greater details later.

Hey! Be honest – what are your reasons to marry?

In concluding, please remember that the success or failure of a marriage depends on the foundation on which the marriage is founded. If Christians will honestly review the reasons behind their choice of spouse they will at least be able to predict how their marriage will look. This can be simply done through self examination and one asking oneself the simple sincere question – 'why do I really want to marry this person?'

Your sincere answer to this question will go a long way in helping you make the right decision in your choice of who to marry.

As you do this, the Holy Spirit will be given the needed chance to step in and convict you of any wrong reasons to marry, re-awaken your conscience and eventually put you on the right pathway to marital success.

CHAPTER 2

BASIC TRUTHS ABOUT CHOICE OF A SPOUSE

The life we live today is a summary of the previous choices we made. And life is a collection of many small and big decisions we make. The importance of the outcome of a decision made will dictate the level of care taken in making such a decision. The decision to buy a white shirt instead of a cream one is a small one as far as I am concerned and I will not be caught spending a whole afternoon tossing that about in my mind. Relocating from my city to another will be expected to take more of my time and thoughts. Not only do I make big decisions with greater personal input, but it will be a smart move to seek advice from other people who know something about such matters, hoping that they can help enrich my decision making process. Also those who will be affected by my decision will need to be consulted. Moving my family out of town will impart my wife and children, and it is only fair and appropriate that I allow them to be part of that decision.

Having stated all the above simple obvious facts, why is it then that the decision to choose a spouse is not treated with the same care and caution as my hypothetical case would have demanded?

The First Step To A Blissful Marriage

Considering the fact that the second most important decision anyone can make is the decision to allow a near stranger into your life, home, finance etc not just for one day or week but for the rest of your life. The most important decision of course is to choose who will rule your life i.e. either God or the devil. Remember none of us is really free in the absolute sense of the word. We are either under the influence of God or of some other gods. Is God your Father, and is Jesus your Master? "…No one can come unto the Father but through me…" says the Lord Jesus Christ. Is He your Lord and Saviour? If you know He is not or if you are not sure please turn to the end of this book now and read a little bit more about the subject.

From the above scenario of relocation, it can be safely assumed that at least those three kinds of considerations should be given to any decision of that magnitude or greater. The choice of a spouse is definitely at such a level. Quickly let us look at the three things to consider before making the important choice of who to marry –

1.   Your decision will affect your entire life

Marriage is designed to complete you and not to diminish you. The completeness we are talking about is not necessarily material, in fact most times it should not be. More often than not we are looking at a constitutional incompleteness in you. I'll give you a good example. I am not very good with remembering names, but I am in a business (ministry) of which the most important skill is relational skill. I mean as a pastor of a church it will help a great deal if the parishioners are referred to by their names and not by some numbers worn around their necks! By the grace of God I will like to believe that I try to relate well in other aspects and areas, but for remembering names. This is a defect that is in my life nonetheless. But, God has made me complete through my wife who is in a class of her own when it comes to putting names to faces. Please do not get me wrong, I did not choose her as a wife because of that. It never crossed my mind that I will ever be a pastor when we got married. But the fact still remains that God in helping my wife and I make a choice, saw the need ahead of time and supplied the resources to meet the need. That is why your prayers must be that God should send to you 'the bone of your bone and the flesh of your flesh'. Look far ahead, think far ahead, and trust the Lord who sees farther than you can see and knows all that you do not know. On your part, it is good to embrace those things in your prospective spouse that you do not have.

2. Your decision will affect your family

Possibly one of the least talked about reasons for failed and failing marriages is the selfishness of choosing a spouse which no one within the family can relate to. Yes I know that it is you that is marrying and not your parents or siblings, but how much shall their feelings be totally ignored? They were in your life up until the moment when your supposedly missing rib or part is found. An important item on the check list of how to know if the man or lady is the right person is this point of seamless integration with the existing family. We are all aware that there are difficult family members who will oppose you anyway, no matter who you introduce to them as your prospective spouse, but that does not remove the fact that your choice of spouse will have an impact on the larger family and their feelings must not be altogether ignored. That is where the issue of parental consent comes in. Do not go with a person who cannot be bothered if his or her parents' consent to whom he or she marries or not. A person who treats his or her own family poorly and can walk away from them without a second thought can also treat you poorly and hence often not worthy of your trust, definitely not of the kind of trust required in marriage.

3. Help is available

'Where no counsel is the people fall, and in the multitude of counselors there is safety' Proverbs 11: 14. Never go it alone! Some people trying to get married swear an oath of silence. Those who suggest such in a relationship are prone to be abusive later. Those who say 'do not let your pastor know about it' or 'you don't need to tell your parents or friends about our plan...'after all you are an adult' are to be carefully watched. If you are not sure, seek counsel preferably from godly people who hold the same spiritual values with you.

4. God is able and willing to guide you.

This in fact is the most important step in making a choice, yet it is one area where people are least sincere. A lot of what we hear as guidance from the Lord is simple self deception. It is not that God does not lead or cannot lead us, but people are so full of their own thoughts and ways much more so that God is just not able to put in a word. Hindrances to hearing God will include:

(i) Noise – When you are hearing too many things from outside (friends, family etc.) and also from inside (fears and fancies)

(ii) Inattentiveness – This is as a result of spiritual sloppiness. Some people will need to be hit in the head and still will not get it. While waiting for God to lead, it is important that you stay sharp and alert.

(iii) Wrong Location – "Seek ye the Lord while he may be found, call ye upon Him while He is near." Isaiah 55: 6. "Behold, the LORD'S hand is not shortened, that it cannot save; neither his ear heavy that it cannot hear: But your iniquities have separated between you and your God, and your sins have hid His face from you, that He will not hear". Isaiah 59: 1 – 2. When you are not in a relationship with God or you have drawn back from following after Him, then His voice will be inaudible to you. If you right your relationship with Him, you will find it very easy to hear God.

CHAPTER 3
IMPORTANT QUESTIONS TO ASK YOURSELF BEFORE YOU TAKE THE STEP

It is suggested that you take note of the answers to the following questions below as important and helpful guidance to making a choice of who to marry.

1.   Do I have a good foundation to base my marriage on?

Choice is the basic foundation for building a marriage.

Wrong/Right choice is like a house built on sandy soil/solid rock. [Matthew 7:24-29]. If the foundation is destroyed what can the righteous do. [Psalm 11: 3]. Please never joke with this issue of choice.

We were involved in counseling a couple sometime ago. The acrimony between the man and his wife was so strong and deep that all those supporting them were ready to give up because no headway was being made at all. A lot of abuse was involved and the civil authorities were already called in. Then as a last push, a group of women went to meet the wife to pray with her and encourage her. During that meeting it was laid on the heart of one of the women present to ask the aggrieved wife: 'what is your foundation like exactly?' That was the point she broke down completely, in apparent sorrow and regret. She went on to confirm that her problems actually started with the wrong choice she made! But praise be to the name of our God who restores.

After much support, the family is now on track. Please get your foundation right! As given to us in the story of the foolish and wise builders in Matthew 7: 24 – 29, it is the rain, the flood and the storm that will reveal the kind of foundation the house is built on. You may wish that there will be no rain, no flood or storm but for your wish to be granted, it might mean that you are located in the desert! Hardly the best place metaphorically speaking, that you will like to have your house located. Even there in the desert, there is storm. The surest way to prepare for the raining day is by building on a sure strong foundation, which in marriage translates to you making the right choice of a spouse.

2.   Am I in a hurry?

Choosing who to marry must not be done hastily.€

Anything that is good and that will last takes time to evolve. The process of choice is one that must not be rushed. The time lost in waiting to make the right choice will pay for itself many times over in the peace you will enjoy in your marriage. Have you considered some of the reasons why medicines/prescriptions, no matter how powerful would have the advice 'if symptoms persist after some days, please see the doctor' attached? Among the reasons is the fact that even the very powerful medicine need to be given some time to work. In fact most of them, the full dosage must be taken over a good length of time for the complete healing process to take place. For example antibiotics are ordered for at least five days to take effect. Do not be afraid of dealing with uncomfortable emotions during that period when you are trying to discover who the right person is. It is better to feel the pain now than later. Marriage is a lifelong project, and great care need be taken before you go into it. Like the computer adage 'garbage in garbage out', marriage adage can go 'rush in rush out'.

3. Am I going into marriage simply out of pity and sentiments?

Choice of whom to marry should be devoid of all sentiments or pity.

If a person will be very truthful with himself or herself, it will not be too difficult to know when he or she is genuinely in love as different from when such a person is only acting out of pity. A pitiful sentiment shows itself in a gentle feeling with a strong determination to rescue the unfortunate. It is the kind of feeling one feels towards a helpless child. It is a cuddly feeling alright, but it is not an appropriate feeling to base the choice of a spouse on. It can easily be confused with love. Yes love it is in a sense, but not the kind of love strong enough to base a marriage upon.

One of the major dangers of marrying out of pity is that when the reasons or conditions causing that pity disappears then the pity will quickly fade away. Also there is a tendency to see the recipient of the gesture of pity as an unequal partner in the relationship. The general attitude will too easily become one in which one party thinks he or she is doing the other a favour. Hence, we hear

Important Questions To Ask Yourself Before You Take The Step [3]

comments like 'I picked you from the dust and have brushed you up......' .....If not that I came to your rescue, I do not know what would have become of you.......'

The truth is, if choice of a marriage spouse is based on pity or favour then there are limited rights. A beggar has no choice the adage goes. Pity is not a good ground to base your marriage upon.

4.   Is Sex the driving force?

Choice must not be made out of lust.

Whenever the overriding reason for wanting to marry someone is to have sexual relationship with that person, then more often than not such a marriage if contracted will not last.

We are talking here of a fixation on that aspect of the relationship. If you barely spare a thought about anything else like, how you will help this person become somebody of significance in life, or how she/he will help you achieve your goal, but you are only full of sexual fantasies about him or her; then I will advise that you do not go ahead.

That strong feeling of lust will suddenly come to an end after a few weeks into the marriage. Amnon a son of David was so 'love' sick that he arranged to have his half sister alone in the room with him so as to violate her sexually. "However he would not heed her voice, and being stronger than she, he forced her and lay with her." And in the following verse the scripture says: "Then Amnon hated her (Tamar) exceedingly, so that the hatred with which he hated her was greater than the love with which he had loved her" [2 Samuel 13: 14 – 15].

CHAPTER 4

WHAT CAN INFLUENCE MY CHOICE?

The Core Influences

Choice brings about change – the choice of the person you marry will influence your future either for good or bad. Choice is part of the blue print that moulds one's life. Whether one chooses to overeat, over drink or oversleep one must remember that there are consequences to the choices made. We live by our choices.

Sometimes one would wonder what exactly young people are looking for in the life of a future spouse that has been barring them from making the choice when it appears that everything is ready. As Christians it is clear that one would not just want to step out based on chance and marry that other Christian even though one may highly esteem the godly virtues manifesting in the person's life. At times one may have the view that God has a specific person ordained for one which is mostly termed 'the perfect will of God'. The choice of that 'perfect will of God' can however be influenced by other factors some of which shall be highlighted soon.

Deep in our subconscious are etched some information which help determine the way our major life decisions are made. These are the core influences which make us look favourably or otherwise at circumstances in the other person's life. The core influences make us take very firm stands which can sometimes be detrimental. God may be steering you towards or away from a particular person and you will just not budge because of the way you see things.

The core influences to a large extent inform how you look at the factors that affect your choice, which will be treated in the next chapter. But for now two things will be identified as core influences on your choice of a spouse.

1.   Taste

It is known that God did leave man's will with him from the beginning. I believe that we exercise this will in legitimate matters through our tastes and style particularly in areas where the Scriptures did not outlined how to go about such matters. Hence even after becoming a Christian and depending on the level of submission to the work of the Holy Spirit, you will discover that you still retain some or most of your tastes particularly towards good things. For instance, ones preference for quality things tends not to change even after becoming a Christian. While one holds the view of getting a superior grade of an item most times backing up one's view with the fact that it will serve longer and better, the other person may just want to settle for the basic version. The person who goes for the cheaper item sees such an item as good value for money while he sees the more expensive item as a waste of resources. Most times it is just a matter of taste.

Equally, as Christians we still make choices based majorly on our convictions, interpretation and the application of the word of God to our circumstances.

However, it is worthy of note that God can use our godly taste and style to guide us in choosing the right spouse.

2. Mindsets

This is similar to the point above and can actually be the end effect of our taste and style over a long period of time. However, our mindset/mentality goes a little bit further to touch things we have always known, accepted as the best and believed to have worked for us most times in the past. These will inadvertently come in when we want to make the choice of a spouse. God's word should govern and overrule our mentality and mindsets. Our mindsets are formed through our past experiences and the experiences of those who are close to us.

Marital experiences of people around us such as parents, relatives and friends can affect our perception of marriage either positively or negatively. Of course, a person's notion about marriage will be positive when surrounded by people with good marriages. On the other hand, people who have been around even so called Christians whose marriages are not worthy of emulation would have a somewhat sour view of marriage. However, it is important to be aware that there are no two marriages that are exactly the same. The fact that marriage was bitter for the other couple you know (whether Christians or not) does not automatically imply that your own marriage will go the same way. In fact allowing the bad experiences of others to influence your choice of who to marry may actually be lack of trust or faith in God to keep and see you through in your own marital journey.

What Can Influence My Choice – The Core Influences [4]

Regarding our personal experiences for instance - A lady who grew up under a burly oppressive father may develop a mindset that will automatically make her to avoid relationship with men who are heavy set in stature. On the other hand we tend to take naturally to people who resemble those with whom we had pleasant experience in the past.

Some people have been exposed to disappointments and hurts from previous courtships or relationships that may come to hunt them and bring bias to their decisions. For example, if someone once had a broken relationship it may be difficult for the person to easily remove the prejudice when someone from the same background or someone looking similar shows up. It is all the more difficult if that same person has had that kind of disappointment and hurt more than once. The person perhaps may have been healed from previous hurts through the word of God but may find it challenging to relate well with a new person having similar characteristics with the previous person.

These influences on our decision making can be very subtle and it helps if we look out for them.

CHAPTER 5

WHAT CAN INFLUENCE MY CHOICE?

Common Issues That Can Make You Pause

The under-listed are some of the common factors that influence the choice of a spouse. Please note that it would be a beneficial exercise to sincerely arrange these items in the order of relative importance to you. In rearranging the list in order of importance to you, number one will be the most important item and eleven the least important. Note also that there is no right or wrong order.

- Commitment
- Love
- Calling, purpose or destiny
- Compatibility
- Material Wealth
- Physical Appearance
- Family Background
- Ethnicity/Race
- Education
- Profession/Job
- Age Disparity

The advice here to any Christian is that you should prayerfully allow God to guide you and also allow Him to deal with the ones adversely affecting you. Please do not 'major in the minors and minor in the majors.'

What Can Influence My Choice? Issues That Can Make You Pause [5]

▸ Commitment

Commitment is very vital because it may be all that will hold the relationship together when the love you once knew seems to be running low. Most times commitment distinguishes the serious minded from the less serious. Have you wondered why couples you see on the streets and bus-stops openly expressing their 'love' for each other end up not marrying each other? More often than not, it is because there is no commitment and they are plain too scared to commit.

Marriage speaks volumes about commitment. All the marriage rites and ceremonies like engagement and wedding are demonstrations of commitment. Ladies in particular should not assume that the man who has been very nice and close to them for a long time intends to marry them until such intention is clearly declared.

The first stage of commitment in marriage is the marriage proposal from the man. The commitment then grows to involve third parties like parents, pastors, friends, the crowd at the wedding ceremony and the acceptance of the marriage vow/covenant, and ultimately staying married for life.

Arguably, if a man is not willing to make the least commitment of marriage proposal perhaps he does not love the woman enough to marry her irrespective of his claims.

It can be said that a few decades ago it was commitment that kept most marriages going. The women were committed to the marriage and stayed even when the going was really rough. The children of such women are eternally grateful to their mothers for forgoing their rights just to see that the children grew up within a marriage relationship. Commitment kept the marriage where the presence of love was suspect.

It has generally been observed that those Christians who are committed to their faith in Christ and to the genuine service of the Lord show more commitment towards their marriage. In a world where commitment is rare, it is time that we the children of God lead the way in bringing this most divine character back for all to see and learn.

▶ Love

If you ask an average person what is the most important criterion for choosing or accepting to marry another person, it is likely you will receive an answer to the effect that 'it is love'. And truly it is and should be in one sense.

If 'love' then is actually behind every marriage why does it all go sour so quickly - at the alarming rate of one in every two marriages? Suppose the love is just the type between two friends or siblings, one would have thought that it would have endured a little longer than some marriages we see today.

It might be right then to ask what *kind* of love is around these days that are so fickle. There are at least four different words in classical Greek meaning different things but are all translated as 'love' in English language, therefore the confusion. So the next time someone tells you 'I love you', it might help to ask...'like how'? Love you like in Eros? - The physical sexual love typically between a male and a female. That is where we get the word 'erotica' from with all its well known connotations. The thing with *eros* love is that it is climactic. It is expendable and once it runs its course it dissipates. It can be built again and again. But if it is the only kind of 'love' that is between two people, *eros* will over time dry up altogether. It is like the sense of smell, which gets used to the fragrance and becomes desensitized. Fresh stimuli are required if one will smell again.

I was once in a perfumery with my wife trying out a few perfumes to buy for our friends. The shop attendant taught us something new that day. After spending a good while smelling different perfumes, she sensed the increasing difficulties we had in making a choice, and so looking at us pitifully the lady graciously handed us a jar of coffee to smell. Why? It was to make our sense of smell sharp again.

The situation many people in marriage find themselves is not much different from that. The fragrance of eros is not enough to keep the love going. You need another different kind of smell altogether to bring the sweet aroma of love back again. That is one of the places where multiple (adulterous) relationships spring from. In relationships based only on the eros, a vacuum may soon be created and because it is essential that the vacuum of love be filled, the person then goes searching because the only 'love' known to the individual is the expendable climactic type of love. Soon and indeed such people fall out of love, erotically speaking, and fall in love with another person often on the same definition of love as the last one.

Thankfully, there are other kinds of love. The *philia* is the kind of love between friends - a kind of 'give and take' love. Where *philia* is genuine, it is of great help in marriage, after all marriage is much more than having a sexual partner as important as that may be. It is a lifelong relationship between a man and a woman who happen to be best friends.

Remember that we are talking about the criterion of love in choosing a spouse, and that our emphasis is on how to be sure of what kind of 'love' you have for someone you are planning to marry and what kind he/she has for you.

There is however a supreme kind of love called *agape*. I personally believe that in the absence of agape it is impossible for anyone to fulfill that 'heavy' stuff in the marriage vow which says 'I do….in sickness or in health, in poverty or in plenty…till death do us part'. Agape has been variously defined as the unconditional love, spirit – level type of love or simply God's kind of love. Staying on the latter definition, it stands to reason that without God, it is impossible to exercise agape in a relationship.

In conclusion, though eros and philia types of love have their place in marriage, however for Christians, these must not be the driving force for the choice of a spouse. It is very important to have the agape type of love and to allow it to drive the entire love package.

- **Our calling, destiny and purpose**

Mostly for the more mature Christians, there is always that underlying awareness of the fact that God will keep using them even in increasing dimension. Hence, they are aware that the person they would marry will significantly impact the accomplishment of the purpose or call of God upon their life.

What Can Influence My Choice? Issues That Can Make You Pause [5]

For example, the awareness of a future ministerial or leadership call on an individual will raise the level of care such a person will take in choosing who to marry. The suitability of the prospective spouse for ministry work is given much attention and carries a greater weight than it would otherwise have carried.

While those around may see a perfect match because of other qualities, the person with a great sense of call to Christian service looks well beyond these other qualities but more closely at the potential for ministry work.

In the same vein, some people factor in the mutual benefit derivable from the union based on the complimentary professions they both belong to; for instance a nurse and a doctor may figure it is easier to start a medical practice together.

▶ Compatibility

Amos 3: 3 says Can two walk together, except they be agreed?
Compatibility is good and many Christians have used this many times as the basis for their choice of who to marry. Using compatibility only as foundation upon which the choice is made however, might not be foolproof.

Human beings are very inconsistent in their ways and it is important to bear in mind that people change both for the better and for worse. The early stages of a relationship are often staged (not intentionally though) because we tend to put on our best manners before strangers and then move naturally into a more relaxed mode when we are with people we are well acquainted with. It is not unusual to hear people scream: "this is not the person I married!" Maybe you never really knew who you married. You might actually be seeing the real person after the marriage. It becomes more painful when the sole basis of the choice which is compatibility is found to be false. The excitement that he or she is very friendly and tolerant of your friends may soon disappear when you notice that it was with a great effort your spouse was carrying on during the courtship, and now he or she just cannot cope anymore.

So if you will use compatibility as an important part of making your choice, allow the Holy Spirit to guide you. Ask that your eyes be open to what you normally would not have seen. Also pray the good prayer: "Lord, grant me the serenity to accept the things I cannot change, the courage to change the things that I can, and the wisdom to know the difference." Compatibility is never 100%. There are areas where you are compatible and there are some areas that you may be miles apart. Some of the incompatible points are changeable, while some are not. Marriage is not designed for one person to change the other into himself or herself, but to grow together. That is why you need to be careful about being too much over the moon in the area of compatibility.

Having said all that, some relationships are so stressful right from the start that it will be foolhardy to go ahead with them.

However, in line with Amos 3:3 and 2 Corinthians 6: 14-16, it is important that two Christians planning to marry be compatible in their belief. It is sad to note that some Christians ignore this major area of compatibility and focus majorly on other trivial areas of compatibility like colours, food, etc.

What Can Influence My Choice? Issues That Can Make You Pause [5]

> **Material Wealth**

Ecclesiastes 7:12 says 'for wisdom *is* a defence, *and* money *is* a defence: but the excellency of knowledge *is, that* wisdom gives life to them that have it.' And in 1 Timothy 6: 13 we are cautioned 'For the love of money is the root of all evil: which while some coveted after, they have erred from the faith, and pierced themselves through with many sorrows'.

Some Christians may claim that they are keeping money in the position it ought to be – servant position and not the master and as such are not influenced by money in major decisions like choice of a spouse. However, we are aware that the best of believers are not exempt from being tempted to seek after money in an ungodly manner.

We may also find that sometimes even very serious Christian ladies who have marriage proposals from many suitors end up using the financial status of the suitors to decide which of the suitors to marry. They may end up settling for the richest or at least the person that has the most lucrative job among them. The point is, if the highly acclaimed and well-meaning Christian people can be tempted with money, then we need to be a bit more careful about how we allow it to influence us.

Money or wealth removes shame, gives some measure of security and comfort, but at the same time can develop wings and fly away. The recent global economic crisis is a good reminder of the fact that irrespective of how well established a person or an institution may be financially, things can still go wrong and really fast too.

The First Step To A Blissful Marriage

Big banks, reputable financial institutions and long standing vibrant business organizations went under because the tide changed. Hence choice based on money i.e. how financially secure a person is could lead to disappointments later in life.

It does not take God long at all to make a man rich, because Haggai 2: 8 says 'all silver and gold belong to me, says the Lord'. And He can transform the economy of a nation in twenty four hours as He did in Samaria in those days when He promised that affordable food will be available by same time the next day.

"I have a message for you. The LORD promises that tomorrow here in Samaria, you will be able to buy a large sack of flour or two large sacks of barley for almost nothing." 1 Kings 7: 1.

And God did as He promised -
"At once the people went to the Syrian camp and carried off what was left. They took so much that a large sack of flour and two large sacks of barley sold for almost nothing, just as the LORD had promised." 2 Kings 7: 16.

▸ **Physical Appearance**

It seems there is a sense of fear that exists among some Christians that God will lead them to 'His will' for them which is a spouse whose physical appearance they will not be able to stand.

Some are so afraid that God will give them a bitter pill to swallow for a spouse that they rather prefer not to involve God in the choice making. They would want to do it all by themselves and just get God's endorsement of the person they have chosen at the wedding ceremony. The default nature of man is to look at the outward appearance, but the Lord looks at the heart. He sees the bigger picture, both inside and outside, present and future. Physical beauty can fade just like a flower. Some people seem to change quickly over time, especially women after child birth.

There may be other changes like disfiguration or deformities through accidents that may mar the good appearance of today, though we pray that this does not happen, yet this is a fact of life.

It is out of poor understanding that some Christians believe that the 'will of God for marriage' is definitely going to be a person that will be very un-attractive. In their thinking, they believe God will do such a thing to them so as to make them 'more spiritual and also to subdue their flesh'. But this assertion is against the nature of our good God and defies the scriptures. James 1:17 says 'every good gift and every perfect gift is from above, and comes down from the Father of light'. Wives and husbands are good gifts and if they are from the Lord, you can count on it that they come in a perfect state. In Proverb 18:22 we are told "He who finds a wife finds a good thing and obtains favour of the Lord". If it is a favour then it must be better than you hope for! That is what the Lord gives, and that is why it is good to trust Him to help you make your choice.

It is entirely wrong and ungodly to assume that God would force you to marry an 'unpleasant' looking person.

To keep things in balance, we believe that while not using physical look as a deciding factor, God will normally lead His child to a spouse that will be pleasant and appreciated. If God is behind the choice, He would have worked on you so that you will see that person who may not be generally too good looking to others, to appear very pleasing to you. After all, beauty is in the eye of the beholder.

It will be advisable to say that one should not go ahead into marriage with someone one is not happy or 'proud' to have as a spouse. That of course is not to say that choice should be based purely on the physical appearance. Remember that all that glitters is not gold.

We can however rest on the fact that God's leading will always lead you to a person that is altogether pleasing to you.

▸ **Family Background**

Undoubtedly, many believers give family background a thorough consideration when making their choice of a spouse even when the person in question is also a genuine Christian. On the other hand, some Christians will only focus on the good Christian standing of the very person they want to marry and will not worry about the family background.

Strong concerns are often expressed in the presence of the following:

- Parents who are divorced or separated

- Addictive behaviours in the family - especially crippling addiction to drugs and alcohol with prostitution

- Presence of genetically transferable diseases like diabetes, mental illness, or even some cancers that have span generations in the family

What Can Influence My Choice? Issues That Can Make You Pause [5]

- Family members with health stigmas like HIV/AIDS

- Family history of worship of false gods, occult practices, and families that belong to other religions like Islam, Hinduism, Buddhism

- Criminal records or notorious ex-convicts in the family

These are just examples of the kind of family backgrounds that may pose some challenges to Christians who would have loved to marry another believer who came from such backgrounds.

There should be no discrimination based on family background as long as the person being considered for marriage is a genuine child of God. We all belong to a new family spiritually and our lineage is now in Christ.

Some subscribe to the view that in some of these difficult family background situations, all you need to do is to be more prayerful, more discerning and be very spiritually alert to do more spiritual warfare in order to break any background link with the devil and keep the devil out of your home.

Remember that Ruth who was from an idolatrous Moabite family was the grandmother of David. Not only that, his (David's) great grandmother was Rahab the harlot. I guess you will not call that a glowing pedigree. Yet out of such an unusual lineage came the Saviour of the world, our Lord Jesus Christ.

However, it is advised that you act in faith when proceeding with a person who has these challenging situations in their family life.

Allow faith to build up in you before proceeding, because 'anything that is not done in faith is sin' [Romans 14: 23]

▶ **Ethnicity/Race**

It doesn't matter if you are a Greek or a Jew, or if you are circumcised or not. You may even be a barbarian or a Scythian, and you may be a slave or a free person. Yet Christ is all that matters, and he lives in all of us. [Colossians 3: 11]

While it is true that some unbelievers have no problem with ethnic or racial differences, unfortunately, it is also true that ethnic or racial difference can be a big problem with some believers especially when it comes to making a choice of whom to marry.

Some believers still hold tribal, racial or cultural values so highly, that they cannot contemplate having a deep relationship with anyone that is not from their own race, or culture.

Such Christians are not prepared to accept any spouse who may not completely share their cultural values.

There is no difference in Christ; once a person is truly born again, he or she belongs to Christ and belongs to the same commonwealth of the spiritual Israel. Extend your right hand of fellowship to people of other cultures in all ways and even in marriage if so led by God.

Allow God to break those cultural biases so that you will not be guilty of exalting your personal and cultural views above the word of God which says we are all one in Christ Jesus.

What Can Influence My Choice? Issues That Can Make You Pause [5]

Some of the cultural issues that separate people are matters that are not insurmountable, like speaking the same language, or sharing similar types of food. If well managed, crossing cultural barriers actually make us better people, as we grow outside of our own 'little' cultures.

Ethnic or racial bias may actually originate from the fact that the person involved holds his/her own ethnic group or race with high esteem while seeing others as somewhat inferior. This bias can grow to outright hatred of other ethnic groups or races. Whatever the case, minor or major, ethnic/racial discrimination is an indication of spiritual un-brokenness.

Some Christians cite the story in the Bible where Abraham insisted that Isaac's wife must be sought among his own people. The point the patriarch was making was that his son must marry from the people of covenant like him. It was more of a spiritual likeness he was talking about rather than an outward ethnic similarity.

Today the people of God are the generality of the body of Christ irrespective of ethnic or racial origin.

If we solely prefer people on the basis of ethnicity or race, then we may be indirectly implying that our own ethnic or racial blood and bonding is superior to the blood and bonding of Christ.

> ▸ **Education**

Some Christians when thinking of the person to marry give some thoughts to the person's level of education for many reasons ranging from compatibility, flow of communication, ability to blend well with their own circle of friends, the trend in the community they live in, their family status, future prospects and opportunities etc.

In some cases this may just be in an attempt to guarantee that their spouse will not be looked-down upon. It is also good to note that 'no condition is permanent' as the saying goes. There have been real life stories of some great inventors and renowned successful entrepreneurs who were not particularly great academically. Some were even school drop-outs. There is also an example of a student nurse that failed the Nursing Council Examination and later became a professor of medicine.

Looking at the bigger picture, there are professors and academic doctors whose marriages and quality of life are not worthy of emulation.

However, there is another group of people particularly men, who will not wish to marry a highly educated lady even when God is them that way. This may be because they feel scared, intimidated or feel their position in the union shall be threatened or challenged if they go into such marriage with such an educated lady.

The obvious truth is that possession of higher educational degrees is not in itself an insurance and security for better and blissful marriage. So, using education as a strong point for choice of spouse may not guarantee success in marriage. If God is leading, then He is able to change the situation and improve whatever educational shortcoming that is in the life of that person you want to marry.

▶ Occupation/Career

Lucrative profession or discipline does not automatically guarantee prosperity. It is the Lord that teaches one how to make wealth. Again, no condition is permanent. I guess all women will prefer their spouse to have the best of jobs.

For some people, the price to pay for having an achiever as a spouse is too much and such people will gladly let go of the benefits so as to spend time together with their spouse. But for those who will rather have the benefits irrespective of the cost, it is but a small matter.

The availability of the wife to help raise children plays more with men and some do factor this in, in their choice of a spouse.

The most important thing is to know who you are and be clear in your mind that you know what you really want; because you will have to live with whatever decision you make.

▶ Age Disparity

Age difference can be of serious concern for some believers at the point of choosing a spouse.

The concern most times is where the female is older than the male or even when the age difference is too small. The basis for such a misgiving is often cultural.

Some concerns may not be cultural in origin, but arise out of a feeling of insecurity. The man may think that a small age gap between him and the spouse may make the woman to be less respectful or be non-submissive. Of course this is not always so.

The First Step To A Blissful Marriage

Respect and submission is not always predicated on age as experience has shown.

Worries about the future physical appearance of the wife do influence the choice of some men. They reckon that women generally tend to age quicker than men and some men have admitted that they do not want a situation where their wife would look like as if she is their mother.

Age disparity may raise some concerns but should not be an absolute criterion in determining God's direction for the choice of a spouse. Either the man or the woman could be older and they can both have a wonderful marriage together.

It is advised however that you have this matter settled in your heart before you proceed, if you have any concerns. The age gap between two people is one thing that will not change. Be ready to deal with the issue in your later life when either or both of you will love to celebrate your landmark birthdays. If it is kept a secret in the early stages of life, it might not be possible to keep it so forever.

The work around for some people who settled for a relationship in which the wife is older than the man is that the wife is allowed to celebrate her landmark birthday anniversaries while the man forgoes his. This is only of relevance in those communities where it is expected that the man be older than the wife.

This should not normally be an issue, but cultures do not change overnight and it is wise to be careful not to strive over issues that do not necessarily contradict our Christian beliefs.

What Can Influence My Choice? Issues That Can Make You Pause [5]

In conclusion, remember that God is aware of all these things that can influence your decision in choosing who to marry - He created you and He knows what you are made of and how best you function.

God is willing to guide you through the right path of choosing who to marry if you will be willing to cooperate with Him.

Once again, be careful that you do not give any undue importance to these issues to the extent that you place career, wealth, appearance etc above what God is saying to you. The heart is deep and only God can know it. Give Him the chance to lead you and you will be glad you did.

CHAPTER 6

THE PLACE OF MATURITY IN CHOICE OF A SPOUSE

We shall start this chapter by asking the question - Are you really ready for marriage? There are a few lessons to learn from the origin of marriage which may help you answer the question. Let us look at the account of the first marriage: the one between Adam and Eve.

Genesis 1: 26 – 27
Then God said, "Let us make man in our image, in our likeness, and let them rule over the fish of the sea and the birds of the air, over the livestock, over all the earth, and over all the creatures that move along the ground."
So God created man in his own image, in the image of God he created him; male and female he created them.

Genesis 2: 15 – 25
Then the LORD God took the man and put him in the Garden of Eden to farm the land and to take care of it. LORD God commanded the man. He said, "You are free to eat from any tree in the garden. But you must never eat from the tree of the knowledge of good and evil because when you eat from it, you will certainly die." Then the LORD God said, "It is not good for the man to be alone. I will make a helper who is right for him." The LORD God

had formed all the wild animals and all the birds out of the ground. Then he brought them to the man to see what he would call them. Whatever the man called each creature became its name. So the man named all the domestic animals, all the birds, and all the wild animals. But the man found no helper who was right for him. So the LORD God caused him to fall into a deep sleep. While the man was sleeping, the LORD God took out one of the man's ribs and closed up the flesh at that place. Then the LORD God formed a woman from the rib that he had taken from the man. He brought her to the man. The man said, "This is now bone of my bones and flesh of my flesh. She will be named woman because she was taken from man." That is why a man will leave his father and mother and will be united with his wife, and they will become one flesh. The man and his wife were both naked, but they weren't ashamed of it.

(a)   Image

It is instructive to note that God created Adam (man) in His image. The realisation of this fundamental truth would have helped Adam to recognise Eve when she was presented to the man. This point is very crucial in the place of choice of a spouse and particularly for men. Many people have image problems or conflict of identity and thus tend to fill in the gap with borrowed images.

This may be one of the reasons why some have an inflated sense of personal worth. They imagine themselves to be what they are not, only ending up as a caricature of someone else's image. It is all about trying to improve their poor self-image and low self esteem.

I remember while growing up how I will put on a particular wrist watch not because of time keeping purpose, but just because I felt it somehow improved my image. I wore the wrist watch over the sleeve of my shirt if I am not wearing a short sleeved shirt, or I would roll up the sleeve for it to be seen! For me at that time, the wrist watch took care of whatever I thought I was lacking in some areas. It was like saying, with this wrist watch, there is no reason why I should not be taken seriously.

To others, it could be very legitimate achievements like academic degrees, successes in career or business that they hang their image on. Achievements and use of trendy materials are good, but deriving a sense of worth and self image from them may be signs of underlying identity problems and issues of low self esteem.

There are instances where young men in an attempt to woo young ladies will go on and on talking about their achievements or even childishly show off the latest fashion accessories or gadgets they possess, often much to the irritation of a discerning lady.

On the other end of the spectrum, are those in whom their low self esteem manifest as pride. This is purely a defensive move on the side of such people. They think it is better to quickly secure the upper hand over other people before they are looked down upon. The problem with such an attitude is that, the contest for superiority is purely in their minds.

One must first realise the image from which he is made which is now found in Christ Jesus. You do not need to carve out any other image. If you are in Christ, you have the best image already. "You are complete in Him, who is the head of all principality and powers" Colossians 2: 10.

I pray you will be able to spot any image problem you may be having as you carry out a self examination.

(b) Presence

Again, until the fall, Adam enjoyed the presence of God regularly. In fact it was during one of those times that Adam was enjoying the presence of God that Eve was presented to Adam. We will recommend that you regularly and genuinely enjoy being in God's presence in order to get the bone of your bone and the flesh of your flesh. God always has wonderful surprise presents for those who spend time with Him.

(c) Not Idle

Adam was not idle in the garden but was preoccupied and diligent in carrying out what he was asked to do. He was tending the garden and naming all the animals. I would rather go with a person who has not got the job of his or her dream, but is occupied with whatever is available to him/her, than pitch my tent with a self-assured dreamer who will not get up to do something.

(d) Ready to Cultivate

As the saying goes, you cannot give what you do not have. We see around us many young people who are not ready yet to add value to their future spouse. The matured Christian, who is ready for marriage is the one who is prepared to cultivate - to plough, plant and grow the future spouse's raw potentials, skills, and innate abilities. It is the person who is able, willing and ready to help the other person in growing the relationship with God and other people.

All aspects of maturity; physical, emotional and spiritual maturities among others areas of readiness have relevance in the choice of a spouse.

A. Physical Maturity

No ideal age is mentioned in the Bible for marriage, but a minimum age of twenty five years for males and twenty one for females are often recommended.

It is widely accepted that females usually mature earlier than males. However, early marriage (teenage) for the female mostly lead to more complications with pregnancy, labour, delivery and eventually huge challenges are faced in caring for the newborn.

Some medical problems associated with pregnancy in young mothers are: difficult and prolonged labour due to underdeveloped pelvic bones, still-births, severe damage to the birth canal and the surrounding organs.

B. Emotional Maturity

As for emotional maturity, it should be noted that age is not synonymous with maturity as there are teenagers with matured approach to life, while there are adults of over thirty years of age who are still teenagers in their emotions.

The Place Of Maturity In Choice Of A Spouse [6]

Marriage is not for boys and girls [Matthew 19: 5]. It is for those who are emotionally mature i.e. a person who is able to guide, lead, comfort and help others. An emotionally mature person must not be sentimental but should be able to manage successes and failures in life. He or she should be capable of making independent decisions of life.

An emotionally immature person drains the strength of those around them.

Signs of emotional immaturity to look out for include:

- **Self-centeredness** - For a child the world revolves around him or her. All conversation and attention must be around the immature person. It is part of our growing up to recognize the presence and importance of other people. The consummate mature Person of all is Christ Jesus who gave up all His rights as God, became a human being and eventually gave up His life primarily for the good of others.

- **The Blame Culture** – A person that plays the victim all the time and who is proficient in the blame culture is not ready for marriage. A common phrase on the lips of a young child is 'it's your fault'. The emergence of this phrase coincides with the stage when the child is trying to establish an identity. Winning is everything for such children. Such behavior is okay for a child, but not for an adult. Frequent crying and other manipulative behaviours like sulking and violence are indications of emotional immaturity.

- **Impulsiveness** – A child will like to buy all the items in the store if you will allow him. The rule for the immature is: if it catches my fancy, I will have it. Such people tend to make a lot of errors of judgment. They take everything by face value. The business of marriage is much more serious than that. Decisions like managing family finance, when to have children and how many to have, where to live and whom to allow to lodge with you requires a lot of calm and prayerful consideration if one will make a success out of marriage and life generally.

- **Tantrums** – This is part of the 'me, me' complex. It deserves a special mention though it has its root in the three characteristics of immaturity mentioned above. An adult may not be caught thrashing about on the floor (though some literally do!), but nonetheless they throw tantrums by being difficult, antagonistic, or disruptive. Inappropriate responses to situations that do not go their way may range from making faces, cruel jokes, sarcasms, sulking, pouting and sniggering right to undisguised direct resistance.

C. Spiritual Maturity

▶ **Should be born again and be led by the Holy Spirit**.

A person who is not in Christ is regarded as spiritually dead. 'And you *He made alive,* who were dead in trespasses and sins, in which you once walked according to the course of this world, according to the prince of the power of the air, the spirit who now works in the sons of disobedience, among whom also we all once conducted ourselves in the lusts of our flesh, fulfilling the desires of the flesh and of the mind, and were by nature children of wrath, just as the others. [Ephesians 2: 1-3].

The minimum standard that a Christian should settle for in the choice of a person to marry is for the would-be-spouse to be born again. Why will the living marry the dead? It is also not good that we give the bread of children to dogs. That is what the Lord says in Mark 7: 27. Also, Revelations 22: 15 hinted the dogs whereas John 1: 12 talks about the children of God. If anyone is in Christ, he is a new creature says the scriptures in 2 Corinthians 5: 17.

▶ Should be on the pathway of holiness

It is not just enough to be a new person spiritually, but it is essential to move onto maturity. The least you should settle for is a maturing Christian. A person who has been born again for many years and has not made any progress may not really be ready for marriage, until a demonstrable effort is seen that he or she desires to grow in righteousness. What bad things he has or she dropped from his or her old life? Marriage is not for babies.

For the man who will be priest over his home, he must be seen to be committed to growth. "It is God's will that you should be sanctified and that you should avoid sexual immorality" [1 Thessalonians 4: 3].

▶ Should be active and useful in the Lord's vineyard

A self absolved person who lives for himself alone is not a good material for marriage. But a person who has the grace and good sense to put his or her hands to work for God is one who can truly be trusted to consider other people in his/her relationship.

An advice for all: Do not out of your selfish desire discourage the person you want to marry from serving the Lord. You may be raising with your own hands a person who will not only turn away from God but turn against you. John 9: 4 says "As long as it is day, we must do the work of Him who sent me (us)" NIV.

D. Financial and Material Readiness

One needs to be financially and materially ready to provide for ones household before entering into marriage. Things like accommodation, household items, a regular source of income should be in place.

Inability and unwillingness to make provision for one's family is regarded as an outright denial of the Christian faith [1 Timothy 5: 8]. Therefore, it is no spirituality at all if a person gets careless with this issue of working to make provision available for the family.

Many have it fixed in their minds how much financially comfortable they must be before marriage. There is no stipulated level of riches that one would need to attain before being ready for marriage. Sometimes, a genuine intent to work towards sufficiency is all that is required.

The majority of people who go into marriage, never have all the finances they would have loved to have before marriage. But a good sign of readiness is hard work coupled with some basic amenities which will give you a degree of independence from friends and family.

E. Social readiness

You may need to search yourself, if you are ready to commit to this person as your best friend for the rest of your life.

After marriage, you cannot just feel like sleeping over with your friend. The kind of accountability required in marriage is of a level that you most probably have never worked with before. Also when babies come, they do have a habit of keeping you awake at night sometimes. The person who objects strongly to having his or her sleep disturbed under any circumstance whatsoever may not really be ready for marriage.

Above all, it is the Lord that we need to look up to for help, so that all the areas of our inadequacy and immaturity can be taken care of by His grace. Are you ready?

CHAPTER 7
AMBER/STOP SIGNS BEFORE YOU GO TOO FAR

Christians are aware that God speaks to us in diverse ways [Hebrew 1:1]. The main challenge, more often than not, is in getting the message the Lord has for us.

It should be noted that it has always been God's practice and character to forewarn His children of dangers ahead. Life is full of traps of the enemy, looming disasters, wrong but good intentioned decisions and many more unplanned bad outcomes resulting from our choices and actions.

You will agree that God knows the very end from the very beginning. In fact one of the best heritages we have in Christ is the privilege of fore-warning and fore-arming. This is even more so in the matter of choice of whom to marry as it a very important decision that affects one for a lifetime. So, the question is; why do Christians end up in bad marriages that are full of troubles and sometimes end in divorce?

In this chapter we will consider some of the common danger signals that may actually be warning signs from God. These signals should not be ignored.

For those who will pause and take good notice of these negative signs when they are present, God in His infinite mercies will rescue them from potential dangers.

Though one may not understand the full reason why a pause is called for, but if one will pray a little more, God would certainly clarify things the more.

Once again it shall be suggested that if you are seeing any of the negative signs stated below, it is advisable that you slow down, pause or stop the relationship completely in order to pray more for clarity as to the way forward. [Proverbs 15: 22].

What some people call 'being madly in love' is nothing but a big accident waiting to happen. It is better to be safe than to be sorry.

Please review the points below as they may be warning - amber lights or stop signs. Prayerfully take each item to the Lord for further guidance.

- **Always arguing or quarrelling**

We know that there are bound to be differences between two people, hence the operative word here is 'always'.

If the frequency of the arguments and quarrels is on the high side, then it may imply that the two will hardly be able to build together.

Frequent arguing, bickering and quarrelling are signs of incompatibility.

Medically, when a person is given another person's organ as a life saving procedure; there is a reaction from the recipient of the organ, called, graft rejection. This is as a result of tissue incompatibility. Except in identical twins, there is always some degree of tissue incompatibility between two people. However in cases of extreme incompatibility between the donor and the recipient, a violent reaction ensues as soon as the graft comes in contact with the recipient's body. The ability to pick the signs and symptoms of early rejection is very essential to the survival of the patient.

In the same way your life may depend on your ability to pick the early signs of 'rejection' in your relationship, and your willingness to do something about it.

A person whose tissue will elicit the least reaction from the recipient is called a 'perfect match'. A lot of effort goes into finding the perfect match. Many tests are run and a careful choice is made before the two body parts are brought together. It is possible to have a perfect match in your marriage as well. God is the perfect surgeon, He did it in the Garden of Eden, He is still working and will work it for you if you will allow Him to help you find your perfect match.

A corollary to the high frequency of quarrelling is the ease with which disputes are settled. When a simple matter of disagreement drags on for days before you come together again, only to repeat the cycle many times, then there are issues.

Again, we are aware that two different people would differ in opinion and disagree sometimes which may even degenerate to quarrel on some occasions.

However it is the willingness and attitude of each party towards the resolution of conflicts that will differentiate a relationship with good potentials from one without.

In situations where genuine love exists, winning the other party's heart is more important than winning the argument or having the last say.

When disagreements occur, are you willing to have it resolved as quickly as possible or will you rather have the matter drag on for as long as it takes for you to win?

Where true love exists between two people, they would rather love to see each other happy and remain in good terms than hold on to some petty arguments over nothing!

▶ **Unreciprocated Love**

Though love is essential for marriage to commence and thrive. A relationship where love is unidirectional is set up to fail before it starts. In our present world where commitment is in short supply it is wise to be sure that the other person has some love for you before you go ahead to marry him or her. Both parties must love each other just as there are two sides to a coin and two cannot work together except they agree.

We have seen cases where people out of naivety and desperation have gone ahead to marry when love was unrequited. They go with the assumption that with time the other person would change and love them back but there is no guarantee that this will happen. In fact it works the other way round most times, the person after staying properly close to you would see more of your shortcomings and more reasons not to love you. Whether you are the one who loves or the one loved, please note that one-directional love is short-lived and cannot sustain marriage for long.

In genuine love there must be the components of affection and compassion instead of mere words and lustful drive.

A good way to look at it is by asking yourself how much affection and compassion does the person claiming to love you have towards your general well-being?

For example, is he or she so obsessed with the so called love that he has taken all your time in a lengthy chat at the expense of the study you really need to do for the examination around the corner?

How much has the person cared or helped you in overcoming that simple challenge facing you? It have been said that 'people don't care how much we know until they know how much we care'.

Trying to impress the other person by your words, ability, or status will not convince a wise person of your love, until the person can see the tangible evidence that you really care. There is a way someone will know if you really have a genuine concern for him or her and if you are making genuine efforts to help.

Be genuine in your love and look out if your prospective spouse is genuine in his or her love. Do not go for anything less!

> **Cannot submit to him (ladies)**

If a Christian lady can hardly submit to the person asking for her hand in marriage irrespective of how hard she tries, then it may be a pointer to the fact that the man may not be the right person. In such circumstances it is important that she allows God to work on her first in this area of submission.

If the unwillingness to submit is due to her status or any other reason then there is need to pause and re-evaluate things.

To submit is to willingly surrender your rights and bring yourself under the other person. It is no longer submission if the forfeiture of right is done under threats and coercion. Men should note this point. If a man has to regularly remind the lady that she needs to let you have the casting vote on a contentious issue, then she might not be for you.

In fact, there are many examples in which one of the ways ladies had a confirmation that the men they married were their right husbands was in the area of their readiness to drop all their defences and ego and submit to the man. Ordinarily, such women would never have allowed any man to exercise such authority over them.

When a woman feels like that (easy to submit) and a man sees such an attitude in a lady, then it is a sure sign that God may be leading them one to another. Where this is lacking however, pause!

▶ **Cannot regard her as a mate (men)**

Christian marriage does not give the man the right to see himself as the boss and take the wife as the servant. Yes there may be hierarchy in the home, but if the man cannot see the woman he wants to marry as a helper and mate then he may have no business marrying her.

The First Step To A Blissful Marriage

When a man has not settled it in his mind to be humble towards his intended spouse irrespective of his spiritual status, career achievements, education, wealth or social status, then such a man should not consider marriage with the lady.

It is not wise to marry someone whom you feel superior to. You may be able to use her for a while, but it is very unlikely that you will love to retain her as a wife for life. 'The servant does not dwell in the house forever...' [John 8: 35]

A man must have it settled in his mind to relate to and treat his intending spouse as a mate, companion, friend, helper, and associate with all equality and respect irrespective of his status.

Whenever a man feels, he is doing the lady a huge favour by agreeing to marry her, then, he is all set to make at least two people very miserable for a long while. The man being one of the two! Spare yourself the pain, pause and see whether you really want to go ahead with this.

> **Superiority or Inferiority complex**

Mutual respect is good and necessary for a successful marriage. However when one party extremely respects the other party to the extent that one cannot freely relate to or express oneself then an unhealthy state of fear is in force. When this is happening in a relationship, it is a sign for you to stop and check.

Someone once cited an example where a well placed single lady in the society (an executive director of her company, who was educated to the PhD level) felt she was led by God to marry her own employee who was her gate keeper. For the pair to enter into this kind of marriage successfully and stay in it; it would be expected that they overcame both inferiority and superiority complexes successfully.

The lady would have had to deal with superiority complex if she had any at all, and in the same breath, the man must have been rid of inferiority complex if he ever had one.

The above example is a testimony to the fact that, it is possible for marriages which some communities will not accept as normal to thrive if the right conditions are present. These complexes are not so much caused by the prevailing circumstances of our lives, but they are products of our different approaches to life. That is, they speak of the way we see things.

If you find yourself in any relationship in which you have an exaggerated sense of being superior to the other person or on the other hand you feel so small and insignificant to the intending spouse, it is a wise to pause and deal with the matter before you go any further.

- **Not being real or being yourself**

Marriage is meant to be a platform for openness and oneness. If one does not feel secure enough to be real and open to the person you are considering to marry then something is not right and this should be taken as a warning sign.

Many people pretend a lot and portray themselves as they are not, for the simple purpose of being accepted.

The First Step To A Blissful Marriage

It is bad enough that one relates to people who are mere acquaintances with such insincerity; but it is inconceivable that a potential spouse should be related to in such a manner.

If the relationship will not survive if the truth is known, then it will not be held together by lies. Acceptance of one another is the bedrock of marriage.

In true love, there should be no need to pretend to be someone different from who you really are. Why will you allow him or her to fall in love with someone else in your name? He will soon discover anyhow that you are not the person he is in love with. It is demeaning to allow yourself to be used as a fodder to feed the fantasy of your intending spouse. Allow the person to come to terms with the real you or else he or she should be allowed to look for the person he or she thinks is right for him or her.

Being oneself does not mean that we should not deal with one another courteously and with etiquette. Some socially unacceptable behaviour should be worked upon, while you are not altogether denying that you have such issues. A person that picks his nose in an unhygienic manner or one that makes so much noise with his mouth while eating, may need to agree to work on these habits, and not just blurt out 'that is who I am'. If you react that way, you may soon realise that not many people are prepared to accept you in such a raw state without making efforts to modify your ways. It is good though if you find someone who will accept you - warts and all, without you having to make any effort to change.

A relationship built on the foundation of lies, spoken to impress will not withstand the rain, the flood and the storms of life. That you are from an affluent family when you are not is not going to help the marriage. False claims of some personal achievements, connections and exploits are grounds on which a marriage that will fail is built.

For example, has he or she been hiding his or her full identity, background, occupation etc?

Even when you ask, does the person beat about the bush and always tries to avoid answering that question? On the other hand, some may release information quickly but it is all lies. There are many wolves in sheep's clothing calling themselves Christians.

Important things that are expected to be disclosed include underlying health conditions, and children from previous relationships.

Believers should pray that God who knows all things and knows the very end from the very beginning will reveal or enable them to know some hidden things about the person they are considering for marriage.

The fear in many has always been that if I let him/her know about that aspect of me, I will lose him or her. This is not love at work. This is taking advantage of someone's lack of knowledge about you so that you can have your way.

True love casts away this kind of fear and goes ahead to put the truth on the table. In essence, the things you fear may bring the relationship to an end if the other person discovers should be disclosed for two reasons.

The First Step To A Blissful Marriage

Firstly, if what exists between you is genuine love, the other party would not back out because of the matter and as such it may become one of the true tests of love.

Secondly, if it would have affected the other party's decision initially, it implies that same will devastate the person later on and it can potentially break the marriage. So why embark on a mission doomed to fail.

When God grants you the benefit of discovering one or two lies that were told to deceive you, it is time to pause and clear things up.

> **Too much effort to make things work out**

Relationships may demand sacrifices but when one party has to be called upon to make near impossible sacrifices just to keep the relationship going then it is time to pause and check.

If all your friends have to be sacrificed, and your career has to be put on hold, while the help you render to your parents has to be stopped, all in a bid to keep him or her, then something is just not right. This is all the more significant if he or she does not need to give up anything of worth for the relationship. Watch out for false trade-ins. A person who says he or she is giving up what he or she never really enjoyed doing for you is not sincere.

On another note, some relationships are filled with too many problems. All sorts of problems are thrown at them from inside and outside. Things are falling apart, and 'the centre can no longer hold'.

This is not to say that if God has approved a journey or relationship then it will be an automatic easy ride. However, when you are dogged with just too many problems in a relationship, God may be sending a warning signal to you through the turbulences you are facing.

As Christians, we have the spiritual power to bind the forces of evil that may face us, but the truth is that you can neither 'bind' God nor 'bind' the storm he allowed for a purpose. The people that were in the same boat with Jonah [Jonah 1: 4 – 16] discovered that fact sooner than later.

It may be best to throw 'Jonah' out of the relationship boat for peace to reign.

If you feel the relationship is draining life out of you, stop and be sure before you go on.

▶ **Looks suspicious to you (difficult to trust)**

Sometimes some people carry on in a relationship when they are clearly finding it difficult to trust the other fellow. It seems as if the harder they try to maintain a healthy trust in the other person, the more impossible it seems to become. As soon as some trust is built, some things happen to destroy the trust.

They may not have all the facts to base their judgement of diminished or lack of trust upon, but it is there.

Whatever be the reason why the trust is not there; whether because you are too suspicious or because truly there is need for real concern, it is important that you pause and set things right (if you can) before you go on. If you are too suspicious you will frustrate the person eventually and the marriage will not be a happy one. And if the person is truly not worthy of your trust, then you will not join yourself to such a person.

- **Inconsistency (today on and tomorrow off)**

Some relationships are riddled with many inconsistencies. One party acts as if he or she is serious with the relationship this week, by next week he or she becomes somewhat indifferent.

This is generally accompanied by failed promises such as unnecessary deferment of the preliminary marital steps such as introductions to family members. On one hand the person keeps postponing the earlier agreed dates based on flimsy excuses and on the other hand he or she tries to make up for previous lapses by committing resources to the wedding arrangement.

This make-and-break kind of commitment may actually be due to some underlying fears. A person that is not sure if he or she wants to proceed may behave like this. The basis for the uncertainty must be confronted if you are the one who is inconsistent.

If you are on the receiving end, try and lovingly find out what the real issue is. Your willingness to let go of the person if he or she does not want to continue may encourage him or her to come clean with you.

- **Over-enthusiasm**

Strange as this may sound, sometimes when one party seems too keen on the relationship, there might be need for you to slow things down a little. The basis is not the enthusiasm which is good, but the underlying 'agenda'.

The person who is very 'excited' about the relationship may act in some ways which borders on manipulation. The danger sign to look out for is subtle or overt pressure. A situation in which you are not given time to make up your own mind about major decisions in the relationship calls for a careful reassessment of things. This is more so when you are convinced you are not being unreasonable by asking for a good measure of time and space.

Subtle pressure may come in form of gifts, services rendered (preparing meals, coming over to help with chores/laundry), and unusual and inappropriate expression of love through words, or even sex.

Some may go into histrionics, like threat of suicide if the relationship is terminated, crying, hunger strike, blackmail and campaign of calumny.

God always gives us the room to make choices, so must you be allowed to make your choice in a God-honouring relationship.

- **Temptation for sex or sexual sins becomes severe and starts to appear unavoidable**

We have earlier mentioned that physical look has a part to play in the choice of who to marry as people should marry who they will be proud of. Physical appearance should not be used as the absolute criterion for the decision though.

The First Step To A Blissful Marriage

Now, as Christians we are also expected to play by the rules and avoid any appearances of evil, e.g. pre-marital sex and its associated fallouts. However, how one chooses to handle physical attraction and its accompanying sexual consequences in a way not to spoil ones testimony is a matter of individual responsibility.

It is a dangerous sign as Christians when one party or both are frequently finding it difficult to exercise the restraint needed to hold themselves from taking 'the honey out of the moon' before the honeymoon.

As car makers have built brakes into cars, so has our heavenly father built into us some braking system to hold us back from crashing.

In summary, it would be un-wise to go on to marry somebody when your mind is not fully made up to do so. Desperation and some other pressures can lead people into this. The scripture in James 1: 6-8, warns against double-mindedness. So the state of your mind on this matter of choosing who to marry is important.

CHAPTER 8

THE CHECK-POINTS

As Christians, we should let the Holy Spirit guide us in our choices as we cannot trust or lean on our own understanding. However, we shall also look at the following checks that will help in making the right choice of spouse. In this chapter, it is suggested that you turn the search light on yourself, and see if you are genuine.

1. Selfishness Check

One of the most crucial concept and basis of marriage touches on companionship and sharing of life together.

Suffice it to say that one of the clearest indications that someone is ready for marriage is the desire to share ones successes, time, belongings, wealth etc with another person – a spouse. If someone is still mostly selfish in thoughts and actions, then by implication, the person is far from being ready for marriage.

The answer to the questions below will assist you in determining where you are in the selfishness check:

- Do you, irrespective of your age admire the blessedness of marriage or better still admire people that are happily married?

- Do you often meditate on or entertain the thoughts of being a responsible husband or wife or mother or father?

The above thoughts and imaginations for example often show a heart that is ready to share and not selfish.

- Do you worry about the idea of another person coming into your life and altering your cherished private life, encroaching on your time and interrupting your enjoyment and fun?

- Are you so engrossed with your personal ambitions and life goals that you are not prepared to welcome anybody into your life, who may alter your plans in any way?

- Do you hold some reservations about marriage because of some challenges that tend to come with it?

These are untold thoughts and feelings that run inside whether we admit them or not but are signs of selfishness.

2. Love-Time Check

True love grows with time whereas mere infatuations weakens or diminishes with time.

Time is the true test of love. There is a greater chance that the strong feeling you have towards the other person is love if it is not transient. Strong, short-lived emotional feeling is more often than not an infatuation.

True love is patient and waits for the right time to express itself fully. Sexual lust wants its gratification urgently and it's not prepared to wait.

Having sex before marriage is not the right way to demonstrate the love you have for one another. It can wait!

3. Love - Singularity & Plurality Check

Often young men and women get to a point where they would find themselves in situation of having more than one person coming to their mind as the likely candidate for marriage.

Christian love extends to all in the family of God, and even beyond. It is not unusual for a man to care about the welfare of many Christian ladies around him. The man will be willing to pray for them, help them and generally be kind to them. However, at the point of choosing a spouse, it becomes a little bit different.

A young man should not have true marital love for both Angela and Juliet at the same time. In the same way, a Christian lady cannot claim she loves both James and John to the point of being confused as to which of the two she should marry.

If this is happening, it is infatuation that is at work, as it can be plural in nature and it is the epitome of confusion.

Confusion sets in when one is not prayerful enough. Genuine love for marriage is singular and not plural.

The advice to give anyone who is not sure whether to marry you or to marry the other person is to ask such a person to go for the other person!

4. Distance Check

This may not apply to many but will apply to those who are in a courtship and they have to relocate. The relocation may be due to a call of duty at work, or for study or for any other legitimate reason for that matter.

Many times people have noticed that their relationship cracked, slowed down and gradually come to a halt shortly after one party relocated.

In some other cases, the relationship immediately nose-dived and came to a sudden end all due to a very recent move by one party. In these cases it would appear as if it was actually close proximity that was sustaining the relationship. Now that one person has moved to a new location, the person sees it as an avenue to liberate himself or herself from the previous relationship which was half-hearted all along.

When you discover that your interest in the relationship wanes quickly after some separation, then it is time to take stock and be sure that you are actually meant for each other. Genuine relationships should survive such necessary periods of separation and thrive well even when there is long physical distance between the pair.

CHAPTER 9

GOD'S LEADING IN KNOWING THE RIGHT PERSON TO MARRY

'The steps of a good man are ordered by the LORD, and He delights in his way' [Psalms 37: 23]. Hence, there is a divine entrance into marriage. Let us look at it this way – If God is the one who truly joins you together, you can be sure He will keep you joined. God being Alpha and Omega is more than able to help you through your marriage. Except by His mercy, God is not obliged to help you progress a project which was all your own idea.

God is interested in and willing to lead you if you will seek His help.

1. God's guidance in making a choice

Looking at the above scripture again - 'The steps of a good man are ordered by the LORD...', please note that this scripture talks about the 'steps' and not the escalator or the elevator, as a man of God once said. If we learn how to allow God to order our steps in our day to day activities, then it will be easy to follow God's step by step guidance in choosing a spouse. It is easier to want to follow the elevator or escalator route instead of the 'step' route.

Many young people irrespective of how well or poorly they hear God, generally will want to hear God instantly when it comes to knowing their would-be spouse. Hence they may resort to many formulae and 'lot casting' or 'fleecing'. This is by no means to suggest that God cannot speak instantly if He chooses to do so but this is just to highlight how we can miss it if we do not wait for God to lead and decide the pace no matter how long it takes. As Christians our lives are supposed to be ordered by God step by step. We shall go through some useful steps that are written in the Scriptures.

God leads mostly through events and substantial signs with vivid and clear confirmations appropriate for your level of understanding and 'spirituality'.

No woozy and fuzzy dreams please...

'For in the multitude of dreams and many words *there are also divers* vanities: but fear thou God'. [Ecclesiastes 5:7].

Remember the three possible sources of dreams and prayerfully find out which one you are dealing with. God speaks through dreams just as our own minds can come up with dreams. There are also demonically inspired dreams which may come as nightmares, spiritual attacks or a decoy. A dream can be a safe method of receiving divine guidance if God has been leading you in such ways before.

Dreams need to be interpreted, and it must be said that the commonest pitfall in dreams for a child of God is not in wrong dreams but in wrong interpretations. How to deal with your dreams is outside the scope of this book but a quick guide for you is this: note as much details of the dream as possible, write them down, pray for interpretation and seek help if need be.

No spiritual bullying and intimidation please...

There are ample evidences to show that some people are coerced into marriage through simplicity of their mind in taking the word of man as the word of God.

We generally suggest that you do not go to a person you like and announce with all authority, "The Lord says you should marry me". And if someone approaches you in such a manner, a right answer for such a person should be: 'that is great, He will be coming to tell me too...once I hear from the Lord I will let you know'. Never allow yourself to be intimidated by anyone and do not intimidate anyone wearing a spiritual mask. A high sounding 'thus says the Lord' wins no heart. It is unwise and sometimes tantamount to simple 'spiritual bullying'. Even the Lord takes His time to woo us into a loving relationship with Him. Be simple, be sincere and be gentle.

No spiritual gymnastics please....

This may come as a shock to some people, who operate by the rule: 'the harder it is, the more likely it is from God'. Nothing can be farther from the truth. Receiving revelation from God for such people must be preceded by a lot of self punishing programs in form of prolonged fasting which may not have been called by the Spirit of God.

Some genuine seekers go on nights and nights of prayer vigil while they are constantly on the edge trying to hear from God. Of course it is good to fast, pray and wait on the Lord, but all these can easily be done in our own power rather than God's and little surprise it often leads to frustration. It is the Spirit that quickens, the flesh (natural ability and ideas) brings no profit [John 6: 63]. Be careful that you do not present yourself as someone who is devoid of all human nature; any half thinking person will see through all the gimmicks and gently pull away from you. Dwell less on those well rehearsed 'spiritual' jargons and let your character speak for you.

2. God's timing for your life (Ecclesiastes 3:1; Proverbs 16:25; Isaiah 30:21)

'Conviction' is key – please remember this.

- ▶ Be Sincere with yourself. God knows!

- ▶ Define your method: Spiritual or 'Egyptian'

No 'shenanigans' please - Don't mix methods (Remember that we cannot play smart games with God See 1 Corinthians 3: 17)

- ▶ Get the foundations right -Solid foundation (Right reasons to marry the person)

There is no typecast method of finding a God-given spouse. God can work in diverse ways and no two testimonies of God's leading in choosing who to marry are exactly the same. However, some basic godly precepts will help. Let's look at the following points on how one may go about choosing a spouse. The list will help us not to set the cart before the horse.

- ▶ Sincere prayers

Many Christians always claim that they have been praying or are seriously in the process of praying concerning making the choice of a spouse. Many back it up with fasting just to demonstrate their seriousness in asking God to guide them. Actually, a good number started praying about whom to marry early enough, probably while still in the secondary school, particularly those who gave their lives to Christ early.

Whether the prayers started early or late as it were, experience has shown that many people do not really know what they are asking for or what they want from God. The real question is 'how sincere are your prayers'?

We have had occasions before in which people were requesting for assistance in prayers for the right spouse. Upon their request they were given blank papers to write down what they want regarding their future spouse. It became obvious that they were not very clear in their own minds what they wanted the Lord to do for them. It is not so much about a long wish list, but about a genuine aspiration for the kind of home you will love to have and that will glorify God.

▶ Observation Period

Allow time to pass on your 'revelations' - It should be a period of observation and not just a time to monitor the person in question from a distance. Observe what God may be communicating through events that may be unfolding. This waiting time is for further prayers and checking with the Lord what He may be saying to you about yourself, your would-be spouse, and even the world around you. A particular Christian brother was once approached by a lady in a particular church and she spoke with him to the effect that he is to be her husband as 'revealed' to her by 'the Lord'. The man took the matter to the Lord in prayers, and promptly the Lord answered him saying the woman is a fornicator and that obviously she could not be his wife. He did not answer yes or no to the lady but allowed

The First Step To A Blissful Marriage

time to pass. It was his observation time. Within three months of receiving a word from the Lord, it came into the open that the woman had actually been living an unclean life and that she was already three months pregnant; all to the surprise of everyone else except this brother.

Observation time is also a time to sift that which is from the flesh from that which is from the Spirit of the Lord.

- Get your conviction(s)/confirmation

This point is fully discussed in the chapter on convictions. It is enough to say here that it is your conviction that will help you hold on when the going goes tough.

During those difficult times, when doubts come in, the only thing you have left is the assurance that God led you into the marriage, and that no matter what, He will see you through it.

- Proposal

With all the care you have taken, the whole effort will only translate into marriage if the person is made aware of your intention. Do not freeze out in fear.

Ideally it is expected that it is the man that should propose to the woman. Adam was the one who excitedly spoke forth saying: I like what I see, let me have it please!

The few examples of marriage proposition given in scriptures uniformly tell us that it is the man that asks for the hand of the woman in marriage. He that finds a wife finds a good thing...The finding is for the man and on the weight of biblical evidence it should be left so. We are aware of the case of Ruth and Boaz in which it was the woman who made the first move and the man then voiced out the words of proposition and endearment. [Ruth 3: 1 – 18].

As previously mentioned, the process of telling the lady your intention should be as simple and sincere as possible. Be real, be cautious. Do not go on too much about the spirituality of the issue on hand. It helps to state with reasonable caution some 'unnatural' circumstances that inform you that the person before you is almost without doubt your would-be spouse.

It is good to sound convincing and confident without coming across as arrogant. Men should know that women universally appreciate a caring, confident, calm and kind man. So, it may help you more if you start as much as possible on a good note. The fact that the Lord says a lady is for you does not mean the person will agree to marry you instantly or even at all. Anyone can turn down a blessing from God. So the battle is not won yet, until both of you sign the dotted lines on the marriage certificate.

* The Myth and the Truth

Some well meaning people hold the wrong idea that the so called 'God's will' concerning who to marry will always be 'a bitter pill' to swallow.

They entertain the thought that the person God will lead them to marry will not be attractive or good looking at all, and that God essentially will make them marry someone they are not excited about.

The First Step To A Blissful Marriage

This apparently, is the reason why some have resorted to avoiding getting God involved in the process of choosing whom to marry. Nothing is farther from the truth!

The real truth about *'God's will'* for anyone is that it is always pleasant and awesome. If you think otherwise please hear what the scripture says in James 1:17 – 'Every good present and every perfect gift comes from above, from the Father who made the sun, moon, and stars'.
The Father doesn't change like the shifting shadows produced by the sun and the moon. [GW].
Also, Proverbs 18:22 says 'Whoever finds a wife finds something good and has obtained favour from the LORD. [GW].

Please note that you have a say in the matter. Even though the Lord is guiding you, He will not take away from you the power to make a choice. This is the pattern in all of scripture. "I have set before you life and death, blessing and cursing: therefore choose life that both thou and thy seed may live." [Deuteronomy 30: 19]
"Look, I'm standing at the door and knocking. If anyone listens to my voice and opens the door, I'll come in and we'll eat together." [Revelations 3: 20]. [GW]
In practical terms we saw from Genesis 24: 57 that Rebecca was given the chance to consent to the proposal from Isaac. "Let's ask Rebekah what she wants to do" [CEV] was the answer of her family members.
Relax; God has good plans for you. When you see it, you will know it!

CHAPTER 10

THE PROCESS OF CHOOSING A SPOUSE

(a) Preparation:

The young women were given beauty treatments for one whole year. The first six months their skin was rubbed with olive oil and myrrh, and the last six months it was treated with perfumes and cosmetics. Then each of them spent the night alone with King Xerxes. [Esther 2: 12. CEV]

But the fruit of the Spirit is love, joy, peace, longsuffering, gentleness, goodness, faith, meekness, temperance: against such there is no law. [Galatians 5: 22 – 23]

Whose adorning let it not be that outward adorning of plaiting the hair, and of wearing of gold, or of putting on of apparel; But let it be the hidden man of the heart, in that which is not corruptible, even the ornament of a meek and quiet spirit, which is in the sight of God of great price. [1 Peter 3: 3 – 4]

A look at the book of Esther shows us that each of the young women selected as the likely candidate for the King to marry, was given a twelve months preparation ritual. The question for us as

The First Step To A Blissful Marriage

Christians today is how much have we allowed the Holy Spirit to prepare us for marriage?

Being a good Christian is the starting point, similar to that in which the young women were selected because they were 'beautiful virgins'. But they needed extra beauty treatment, pointing to the fact that our character flaws and bad habits need to be worked on and treated by the Holy Spirit before marriage.

We must allow Him to bring out in us the fruit of the Spirit and adorn us with unfading inward beauty as a necessary preparation for marriage.

b. Seeking: (Matthew 7: 7, 8, 11; Deuteronomy 4: 29)

Ask, and it shall be given you; seek, and ye shall find; knock, and it shall be opened unto you. [Matthew 7: 7]

But if from thence thou shalt seek the LORD thy God, thou shalt find him, if thou seek him with all thy heart and with all thy soul. [Deuteronomy 4: 29]

"He that finds a wife, finds a good thing..." Seeking must precede finding.

The art of seeking required is akin to that of a skilled hunter who uses all his senses to pick up the slightest right signal. What many call seeking in relation to marriage is more of a blind, desperate and often fleshly attempt to grab anything and everything that comes their way. Seeking without godly skill is frustrating and futile. The psalmist says "He teacheth my hands to war, so that a bow of steel is broken by mine arms." [Psalm 18: 34]. A person that is taught of the Lord in the art of searching for a spouse is able to use his dreams, join them with a word from the pulpit, and skilfully match all with the person standing in front of him.

Seeking demands time, energy, wisdom, discretion, consideration and patience. Seeking calls for careful, diligent, and persistent effort of application.

How Do I Seek?

▸ Get busy in the Lord's vineyard.

Delight thyself also in the LORD; and he shall give thee the desires of thine heart. [Psalms 37: 4]

▸ Set godly, modest and unbiased standards.

Behold, I stand here by the well of water; and the daughters of the men of the city come out to draw water: And let it come to pass, that the damsel to whom I shall say, Let down thy pitcher, I pray thee, that I may drink; and she shall say, drink, and I will give thy camels drink also: let the same be she that thou hast appointed for thy servant Isaac; and thereby shall I know that thou hast shewed kindness unto my master. [Genesis 24: 13 – 14].

Abraham's servant who served as his go-between had an idea of the kind of wife that will be best for his master's son which will also be pleasing to God.

You are allowed to dream and have desires, but just make sure that they are godly standards. It is okay to purpose in your heart that you will not settle for anything below a particular level morally.

▸ Have specific desires, but don't be rigid.

Let God have His way. The balance to the point about standard made above is that you should always be prepared to let God have His way. The person you eventually get may not fit the bill immediately, but rather grow into it. The process of becoming what you desire then becomes a joint venture between you, your spouse and God. Sometimes it is sweeter that way. The rough in the diamond kind of person, has its own blessing as nothing gives us joy like witnessing the birth of a new thing. Better still, it is great to be part of the process of bring life to the world.

Every way of a man is right in his own eyes: but the LORD pondereth the hearts. [Proverbs 19: 21]
There are many devices in a man's heart; nevertheless the counsel of the LORD, that shall stand. [Proverbs 21:2]

c. Look:

Have fellowship with God's people; attend living churches, Christian fellowship meetings, camp meetings, conferences, Holy Ghost Services and Retreat programs [Hebrews 10: 25] though not with the sole intention of getting someone to marry to the point of missing the spiritual blessings there-in. God will prompt you to look at His beautiful children and He will show you the particular one that is yours.

d. Wait:

Once you see that which is good, do not jump into conclusion like Samuel did in 1 Samuel 16: 6 "And it came to pass, when they were come, that he looked on Eliab, and said, Surely the LORD'S anointed *is* before him." Only to be told by the LORD "...Look not on his countenance or on the height of his stature; because I have refused him: for *the LORD seeth* not as man seeth; for man looketh on the outward appearance, but the LORD looketh on the heart." [1 Samuel 16: 7].

David eventually was brought to Samuel and God told him to choose David as the right person. *And the LORD said, Arise, anoint him: for this is he. Then Samuel took the horn of oil, and anointed him in the midst of his brethren: and the Spirit of the LORD came upon David from that day forward. So Samuel rose up, and went to Ramah.* [1 Samuel 16: 13 – 14]. Wait for your David and you will be glad you did.

Wait for the right person through your closet prayers, specifically asking God for direction regarding the brother or sister. In other words be very prayerful. Please wait on God in prayer and even in fasting if you so wish.

e. Listen:

When you wait on God and wait patiently, the Lord will lead you through any of the following ways: Inner witness or still small voice as Elijah was led in 1 Kings 19:12-13. Proverbs 20: 27 also says 'The spirit of man *is* the candle of the LORD, searching all the inward parts of the belly'. An audible voice as Samuel heard in 1 Samuel 3: 1-4 is another way the Lord can communicate His will in marriage for you. Other forms of divine leadings are through the word of knowledge, dreams, visions and revelations and godly counsel through pastors and other Christians.

CHAPTER 11

CONVICTION

Earlier on in chapter five, we looked at the factors that commonly influence a person's choice of a spouse.

All the factors listed in chapters four and five, in one form or another influence the eventual decision made. Having weighed the evidences, a person comes to a place in his mind when he or she thinks; this is the way I want to go. The sum total of those points or factors is what is called the person's conviction.

The word conviction is the noun of the action word (s), 'to be convinced', which means "to bring by the use of argument or evidence to firm belief or a course of action"

Conviction means - to prove adequately and not entertain any doubt, fear, conflict or contradiction. It is a strong belief of being right, accompanied by an inner satisfaction that the course of action taken or about to be taken is the right one.

Conviction is a highly individual thing. It is not about convincing someone else about your course of action, but it is the ground upon which your decision was made. You should be able to look at yourself in the mirror and say, 'to the best of my ability and understanding, I am making this decision'

Conviction [11]

Your conviction is the truth you hold on to as a proof that the Lord has spoken to you about or guided you into a marriage relationship. It is the foundation on which your decision is built. Many things may be pointing to a person, but there is an overriding proof that the relationship has the hand of God in it. Your conviction is what will keep you going when the going gets so tough and would provide the answer you need when you begin to wonder if you made a mistake all along in marrying the person. You can see how important your conviction is now. It is not something you made-up as that will only amount to self deception.

Your conviction is not given to you by God just for you to use to convince your pastor or parents, but it is for you! Be true to yourself. Because we are prone to mixing up what is in our spirit with what came from our untransformed soul, it is important to leave yourself with a little chance that you may not be hearing hundred percent from God. That is why it is helpful that you have your revelations confirmed by other means apart from the primary channel through which you believe the Lord spoke to you in the first instance.

▶ **We need Conviction:**

- Because marriage is for lifetime.

- So that our minds will not be tossing around during courtship and in marriage contemplating mistakes made or regrets.

- So that we can fall back on it when challenges come in the marriage and in the future.

- So that we can enter and enjoy God's rest.

HELPFUL ADVICE

- The important choice of who to marry is a personal and independent decision which should be taken in the face of multitude of godly counsels.

- You are responsible for your decision.

After establishing God's perfect counsel on who to marry:

- Be willing to subject the intending relationship to scriptural yardsticks and scrutiny

- Faith and agreement are necessary

- Conviction and love are fundamental (be fully persuaded in your mind)

- Peace is confirmatory.

There is a peace which comes from God that accompanies a right action. The peace from God must be differentiated from the sense of security that follows some pleasurable things a person may be engaged in. Enjoying a sexual relationship with a person you may not marry may feel like peace, but it is only a false sense of security.

CHAPTER 12

TO WHAT EXTENT CAN I BE SURE THAT I AM RIGHT?

We have discussed the importance of having a strong personal conviction about who to marry. It is however a necessary step of wisdom to know that no matter how sure you may think you are, there is still a chance that you may not be right.

Many well meaning, but ill informed Christians have gone ahead into marriage expecting great results based on their convictions, only to discover that the reality of their marriage does not match the certainty of their decision. They were so sure (and sincerely too) going into the relationship, yet it has now all turned sour.

A closer look at such cases which unfortunately are not rare will reveal that they missed one important step. And that is the step of double checking their convictions with others. It is good to be sure, but it is better still to be cautiously sure. Micah 6: 8 says God desires that we walk"....humbly with Him". A person walking humbly with God will have the mindset of the apostle who says in Romans 3: 4 'let God be true but every man a liar'. By implication, always reserve that small percent chance of not hearing correctly. All who approach marriage this way are rarely wrong in their choice.

The First Step To A Blissful Marriage

Can you match these credentials?

- Pledged to God before conception.

- Conceived through a fervent request to God.

- Completely consecrated to God about the age of one.

- Lived in God's premises throughout childhood.

- Was under the tutelage of an experienced high priest throughout his growing up years.

- Learnt the way of God and how to hear God from a very young age.

- Rose to become a renowned national prophet of God.

- Used of God in important assignments – including the ordination of the first king of Israel.

- Had none of his 'words fall to the ground' - All his prophecies came to fulfilment.

- Heard God and declared God's position on the rejection of the first king of Israel.

- Sent by God Himself to go and anoint someone in the house of Mr. Jesse.

- Heard from God not long ago – possibly earlier that same day.

- Can we say - became an expert in hearing God.

To What Extent Can I Be Sure That I am Right [12]

Yet he got to Mr Jesse's house and got it wrong seven times.

The outline above is an excerpt from Samuel's life.

Prophet Samuel was a reputable man of God, an expert in the art of hearing God. One day he arrived at the house of Jesse to carry out an assignment given to him by God... [You can read the full story in 1 Samuel 16: 1 – 13.]

There are important lessons to learn from this account in the scriptures.

1.   *Do not base your decision purely on past experiences.*

What made Samuel to think that Eliab is the chosen of the Lord?

Eliab appeared physically well-built just like Saul whom Samuel anointed king the last time. The prophet's thinking apparently was that, the last time I was sent on a similar errand by the Lord, these were the criteria, and so it must be now.

Our previous experience of how God leads is good but using such experiences to conclusively make subsequent decisions can be misleading. We cannot stereotype God. He works in diverse ways.

Also Samuel could have picked Eliab because he saw Saul in him. Let's explain. Samuel loved Saul a great deal, and he would have loved to see him make the best of the opportunity given him to be king over Israel. In the first verse of the sixteenth chapter of the book of first Samuel, God essentially had to tell Samuel to move on from Saul. He was too emotionally involved with the first and only similar decision of anointing a king for Israel. The lesson – Be careful not to place too much value on an experience you gained from a previous decision which you have not fully recovered from.

For example, it is easy to be misled by going into a relationship with someone who resembles the person you last had a relationship with. Especially if that relationship ended on a note that leaves that person's image untarnished before you.

The credentials of spouses you were separated from through death and failure to secure parental consent are typical examples of past experiences that need not be necessarily deployed again.

2.   *There is always something more than you are seeing at the moment.*

Why did Prophet Samuel think that he had to choose only from those presented to him? He probably forgot that there is always more to God than meets the eye - more to Him in nature, more to Him in provision.

No matter how deep we think we have gone in our walk with God, we are still men and we must recognise that there is more to God and His provision than that which is placed before us. When a person looks around and says there is no way I can find anyone to marry here, it is clear that such a person has forgotten that David is in the field and he could easily be sent for. Stories of provision of wonderful spouses abound following sudden relocation of the man to where the lady is placed and vice versa.

To What Extent Can I Be Sure That I am Right [12]

Trust in the LORD with all thine heart; and lean not unto thine own understanding.
In all thy ways acknowledge him, and he shall direct thy paths.
[Proverbs 3: 5 – 6]

3. *Do not settle for anything because you have been wrong too many times*

Why did Samuel make the same mistake seven times?

For an experienced prophet like Samuel, making a mistake once, twice or three times is bad enough, but making the same mistake seven times within a short period of time is to say the least unacceptable.

But that is where the virtue lies for this great man. He did not just make something up to save his face, but rather he went on trying until he eventually got it right.

Do not settle for your mistake. After you have spoken to your pastor and parents the fifth time saying 'thus says the Lord', and you discover that it is not looking good again, please do not grit your teeth and go ahead to marry the person. She is simply your sixth mistake, and that does not make her any better than the previous five mistakes. A mistaken conviction is a mistake and a mistake in marriage is a disaster! You cannot qualify it in any other way.

4. *No one is infallible except God*

Let God be true let all men be liars - I have often heard people speak about how they so much trust the judgement of other respected Christians; which is good. But remember that they are still men and the possibility of getting it wrong is always there. So trust God more to give you the correct revelation of who to marry.

CHAPTER 13

WHAT SHOULD I DO WHEN HE/SHE IS NOT WILLING TO MARRY ME?

The Jonah Spouse And The Elijah Spouse

Many young Christians that went through pre-marital course at different times have always asked the question: 'What if I have a strong conviction that I believe is from God (and such conviction has even been confirmed by God through other respected Christians e.g. pastors) that a person is my future spouse but then the person is not willing to marry me?'

As Christians we shall try to answer this question through the viewpoint of the supremacy of God. God cannot lie and also His purpose cannot be thwarted by any man. We shall look at this with a few examples in the Bible that we could draw some lessons from.

Take note of the following scriptures as we try to answer this question.

Numbers 23:19 - *God is not a man, that he should lie, nor a son of man, that he should change his mind. Does he speak and then not act? Does he promise and not fulfil?*

Amos 3: 3 - *Can two walk together without an agreement?*

The First Step To A Blissful Marriage

Proverb 21:1 - *The king's heart is in the hand of the LORD, as the rivers of water: he turns it wherever he wishes.*

Romans 3:4 - *Not at all! Let God be true, and every man a liar. As it is written: "So that you may be proved right when you speak and prevail when you judge......"*

The Jonah Spouse

This title – the Jonah spouse has been chosen by the reason of how we can use the lesson learnt from the story of Jonah (though not a marriage story), to illustrate our answer. We can apply the principle in the story to the choice of a spouse. There are a few more biblical examples where God would set aside a person's position and put in place His own plan, all for the person's good. The stories of the Shunammite woman and Elisha [2 Kings 4: 8-17], and Zacharias and the angel [Luke 1: 11-24] are other examples.

The Shunammite woman did not want a baby and was even sceptical of the prophetic declaration of Elisha, but all the same God out of His mercy ignored her doubts.

God also ignored Zacharias' unbelief and went ahead to give him a son - John the Baptist who was the forerunner of Christ.

The story of Jonah is more vivid as Jonah tried very hard to run away from God's intention and assignment. However, Jonah did not have a problem of doubt. He did not struggle with the thought of whether it was God giving him the instruction or not, but he was very resolute anyhow that he will not go the way God wanted him to go.

He had his own reasons that appeared good in his eyes. Jonah felt that it was right for God to punish Nineveh and he would not have it any other way. It is instructive to note that irrespective of Jonah's resolution not to do what God wanted; God eventually prevailed and still got Jonah to do the job.

In case of choice of a spouse, some good Christians may be resisting God's leading even when they may be aware that the hand of God is on it. Like Jonah they may have in their mind what seems to them as a very good and justifiable reason to explain their position. The 'Jonah spouse' in this case would be those who through God's exceptional mercy would be re-directed by God to go the way He wants them to go. This is by no means to suggest that God is a bully but just to demonstrate His supremacy, sovereignty intertwined with His exceeding love towards man particularly when His purpose is at stake. The Jonah spouse would eventually be brought to marry the "God's will" irrespective of how much he/she tries to resist doing so. This is more so in those situations where God has a plan to use the union for His work on earth.

The Elijah Spouse

This is the other side of the coin and it is meant to show that no man is indispensible when it comes to doing what God wants done. No man can hold God to ransom.

Elijah has been regularly led and directed by God, but following some threats from Jezebel that she would kill the prophet, Elijah got tired of the whole business and he in turn threatened to quit being a prophet.

The First Step To A Blissful Marriage

Elijah was no longer willing to continue to be used of God and actually wanted God to take his life away. He had actually thought that he is the only one remaining and had complained to God about it.

He continued to show his reluctance to continue with God's business. And God's response to his repeated complaint was to provide two auxiliary replacements; Hazeal and Jehu and one full-time replacement for him – Elisha. God also made him aware of the fact that there were 7000 substitutes or potential replacements.

The Elijah of a spouse can be described as that Christian who may willingly want to opt out of the leading of God regarding the choice of who to marry even when he or she is sure God is leading him or her that way. Such a person is always substituted with another competent replacement by God.

God will also demonstrate to such a person that He has more than enough substitutes - up to 7000 replacements in the person's stead.

Because God cannot run out of resources He would bring another faithful Christian to marry the person that the 'Elijah spouse' is failing to marry for fear of whatever he or she is seeing as a threat towards accepting that godly choice.

There have been cases where some people will not just give up on a person who is already married because they hold on to a previous revelation that the person is their future spouse.

They still go ahead praying that God would change the situation and still bring the person back to marry them. Unbelievably, some we learnt had prayed that God would either break the existing

What Should I Do When He or She Is Not Willing To Marry Me? [13]

marriage or kill that spouse that had taken 'their place' so that the man or woman in question would be freed to come back to marry them.

Well, the would-be-spouse you think that is clearly God sent may fall into this category we have described as the 'Elijah Spouse'. You need to move on with the Lord even when you strongly believe He brought that 'deviant person' who refused to marry you. In this case, you would be wasting your time and hindering your progress by hoping for a come-back.

Please note that immediately Elijah left the scene spiritually, Elisha showed up. Don't keep waiting if the person has reached a point of no return – married to another person. Better still; don't keep trying to coerce the unwilling Elijah spouse to marry you even when you think God's hand is on it. You may well be preventing your 'Elisha' from showing up.

Another interesting thing with this metaphoric 'Elijah Spouse' analogy is that the 'Elisha' would eventually and always be twice as anointed as the 'Elijah'. Hence, the 'Elisha' when allowed to show up would be twice endowed as a spouse than the previous unwilling 'Elijah' person. Many married Christian couples would attest to this fact - that they once felt God was leading them to a person to marry but the person was somewhat unwilling and later they got a spouse far better than the unwilling person.

CHAPTER 14

MAJOR CHALLENGES OR OBSTACLES TO CHOICE OF WHOM TO MARRY

Sometimes, after a Christian has obtained what can be called a strong conviction from God regarding whom to marry, the person may face situations that strongly challenge the original conviction.

Even the very tenacious and ardent in faith may be shaken by the challenges we will mention below. These challenges to varying extents can cause the individual to reconsider the decision to marry the person hitherto believed to have been approved of God.

- ▶ Genetically inherited conditions (Sickle Cell Disease, Thalassaemia)

- ▶ Serious Conditions (Deformation due to accident, No womb, No menstruation, No erection etc)

- ▶ Terminal illness (Cancer, Leukemia etc)

- ▶ Stigmatized terminal illness (HIV/AIDS etc)

- ▶ Strong Parental Objection (The strength of this challenges varies with cultures)

Major Challenges Or Obstacles To Choice Of Whom To Marry? [14]

Genotype

There have been several cases where two people are convinced that they want to marry each other but are facing challenges based on their genotypes.

The common area of challenge is with sickle cell anaemia. The one in four statistical chances that a couple with blood genotypes AS will produce a child with sickle cell disease is a big challenge to face. Some would want to look at it with the eye of faith and would want to go ahead with the marriage. For others, the discovery that there is a chance for such an occurrence marks the end of the relationship irrespective of their previous convictions.

Serious Underlying Conditions

Some underlying conditions such as damage to the womb, absent menstruation, and impotence may present challenges to the other person who may have agreed to the marriage. However, we encourage that these conditions should be disclosed prior to marriage though the information has to be well managed by the other party.

If these matters are not disclosed at the onset but found out later in marriage, the un-affected party may feel betrayed and trust may become difficult to build again. Put yourself in the position of the other person, how you will feel if you are on the receiving end.

Terminal Illness

The thought of loosing someone not too long after marriage due to a terminal illness that has been diagnosed such as Cancer,

Leukemia etc could pose a very serious obstacle to the decision to marry the person. Some believers who faced such challenges did sincerely direct their faith and prayers towards the healing of such persons. The best outcome is to have the person completely healed so that both of you can be healthy to enjoy the future marriage.

Stigmatized and Communicable Serious Illness

HIV/AIDS is an example of such illnesses that are serious, transferrable and stigmatized in most of our societies. Hence when a young person about to marry discovers that the other person has such an illness, it becomes a very strong challenge to the decision. In all cases of illnesses, communicable or terminal, prayer for healing is foremost encouraged and godly counsel strongly recommended.

Strong Parental Objection

Though secularization has tampered the effect of parental objection in some societies, it is still very strong in some cultures. In the cultures where this is still a major issue, refusing to heed the instructions of the parents not to marry a particular person may altogether be seen as a direct disobedience to God. This has been a serious challenge to Christians in such communities.

Let us not throw away the baby with the bath water – God can also use the stance of godly parents to guide their vulnerable Christian children from getting into trouble by marrying the wrong person.

Demarcations however must be made between unreasonable and selfish interest of the parents, and an objective disagreement with the ward.

Major Challenges Or Obstacles To Choice Of Whom To Marry? [14]

In some cultures, parental influence can be very strong especially where parental consent is accepted as a pre-requisite for marriage. In such cultures, the life of a young person can literally be torn apart because; he or she is not allowed to go on with his or her life simply because the parent will not consent to his or her marriage.

Most Christian churches and cultures encourage parental consent before marriage. However some parents have used this as an opportunity to set racial, ethnic, cultural, geographical, political and social boundaries outside of which their child cannot marry.

Sadly, some Christians have made wrong choices just in the bid to please their parents. For example, some have married unbelievers from a particular family, town, or caste just because they want to please their parents. In such cases the idea of finding out God's position regarding the choice was completely out of the question. Even as we speak there are some unmarried mature Christians from these backgrounds who are sincerely searching for whom to marry but cannot dare mention the probable right candidate to their parents: All just because their parents cannot imagine their own child going outside of the set boundaries to marry from the 'other side'.

Unfortunately such children of God are forced to restrict their search or 'prayers' for 'God's will' to the areas defined for them by their parents. A person in that kind of condition is not open to any leading from God that is not in line with what their earthly parents have laid down for them.

The First Step To A Blissful Marriage

Ironically though, these parentally imposed boundaries do get widened by the parents themselves particularly for their daughters when time seems not to be on their side anymore.

There are some other cultures in which the parents are the ones to find and decide who their daughter or son will marry. This is sometimes called 'arranged marriage'. Whichever culture you belong to, as a Christian, please do not marry to please any man.

The general advice towards these challenges is that you should go as your faith can carry you. Take a stand and keep praying ahead of time.

CHAPTER 15

HELPFUL AND RECOMMENDED APPROACHES TO PROPOSALS AND RESPONSES

Marriage proposal and acceptance of the proposal are all very necessary to begin a marriage relationship. None of these suggestions is cast in stone. Common sense, good manners and genuineness will help you secure your cherished spouse to be after you have received your conviction.

Below are few recommendations that have been proven to be very helpful.

- Men! Inform your pastor/Christian leader after you have prayed through.
- Men! Be gentle, polite but straightforward and resolute during proposal.
- Men! Avoid saying, "Thus saith the Lord". Let your approach be natural.
- Men! Do not hurry the lady to decide fast. Give her enough time to confirm your 'revelation'.

*No 'bullying'! No 'intimidation'!

The First Step To A Blissful Marriage

- Ladies! Do not delay the brother's answer as soon as you've gotten one.

- Ladies! Check proposals with your heavenly father before going further.

- Ladies! Never 'manipulate' or 'work on' the brother in order to squeeze out the proposal

- Ladies! Please don't be snobbish.

- Men! Leave room for refusal, but don't give up easily if you are very sure.

- All! Pray, watch and act wisely.

THE FIRST CHOICE

This book has been written primarily with the Christian person in mind. The principles and guidelines in this book will work best for a person who subscribes to the Christian ethos.

The uniqueness however of the Christian faith is that Christianity is not a set of rules and instructions, (there are instructions and rules of course as we are not lawless) but a relationship with a Person, Jesus Christ.

Going to church does not make you a Christian, just as living in the palace does not make you a prince. You are only a prince or princess because you are born by the King.

Are you born of God? Can you truly and sincerely say that you are spiritually born of God? Is God your Father? If not, you can become a child of God today. You can be born again.

A few simple steps to become a child of God and make the principles in this book work best for you are:

Acknowledge your sins and ask that the Heavenly Father will forgive you. Believe that Jesus Christ came to die for your sins and reconcile you back to God. Confess Jesus Christ as your Lord and Saviour and ask Him to come into your life so that you can have a personal relationship with Him.

BIBLIOGRAPHY

1. To Have And To Hold Forever, 2000 RCCG Acme Ogba
2. http://marriage.about.com/cs/engagement/qt/reasons.htm
3. http://www.thefreedictionary.com/convince